The Miniature Schnauzer

Our Best Friends

OUR BEST FRIENDS

The Miniature Schnauzer

Janice Biniok

ELDORADO INK

Produced by OTTN Publishing, Stockton, New Jersey

Eldorado Ink
PO Box 100097
Pittsburgh, PA 15233
www.eldoradoink.com

CPSIA compliance information: Batch#101909-5. For further information, contact
Eldorado Ink at info@eldoradoink.com.

First printing

1 3 5 7 9 8 6 4 2

Library of Congress Cataloging-in-Publication Data

Biniok, Janice.
  The miniature schnauzer / Janice Biniok.
      p. cm. — (Our best friends)
  Includes bibliographical references and index.
  ISBN 978-1-932904-61-1
  1. Miniature schnauzer. I. Title.
  SF429.M58B56 2010
  636.755—dc22

                              2009041442

Photo credits: © American Animal Hospital Association, 75; © istockphoto.com/abishome, 54;
© istockphoto.com/bedo, 69; © istockphoto.com/lauradyoung, 37; © istockphoto.com/
MarkCoffeyPhoto, 93; © istockphoto.com/s5iztok, 90; © istockphoto.com/Simon_I, 67;
© istockphoto.com/theboone, 27, 48, 98; Jon Oakley (http://www.flickr.com/photos/jono2k5/
101294111), 53; © 2009 Jupiterimages Corporation, 34; Library of Congress, 22; Courtesy
National Association of Professional Pet Sitters, 96; Used under license from Shutterstock,
Inc., 3, 8, 11, 12, 13, 16, 18, 19, 21 (all), 23, 28, 31, 32, 36, 38, 40, 41, 43, 45, 46, 47, 50, 51,
58, 59, 61, 71, 72, 74, 76, 79, 80, 82, 85, 86, 88, 94 (both), 95, 97, 110, front cover (all), back
cover; Diane Ykelenstam, 57, 62, 63 (all), 64 (both), 65 (all), 66.

**For information about custom editions, special sales, or premiums,
please contact our special sales department at info@eldoradoink.com.**

TABLE OF CONTENTS

Introduction

GARY KORSGAARD, DVM

The mutually beneficial relationship between humans and animals began long before the dawn of recorded history. Archaeologists believe that humans began to capture and tame wild goats, sheep, and pigs more than 9,000 years ago. These animals were then bred for specific purposes, such as providing humans with a reliable source of food or providing furs and hides that could be used for clothing or the construction of dwellings.

Other animals had been sought for companionship and assistance even earlier. The dog, believed to be the first animal domesticated, began living and working with Stone Age humans in Europe more than 14,000 years ago. Some archaeologists believe that wild dogs and humans were drawn together because both hunted the same prey. By taming and training dogs, humans became more effective hunters. Dogs, meanwhile, enjoyed the social contact with humans and benefited from greater access to food and warm shelter. Dogs soon became beloved pets as well as trusted workers. This can be seen from the many artifacts depicting dogs that have been found at ancient sites in Asia, Europe, North America, and the Middle East.

The earliest domestic cats appeared in the Middle East about 5,000 years ago. Small wild cats were probably first attracted to human settlements because plenty of rodents could be found wherever harvested grain was stored. Cats played a useful role in hunting and killing these pests, and it is likely that grateful humans rewarded them for this assistance. Over time, these small cats gave up some of their aggressive wild behaviors and began living among humans. Cats eventually became so popular in ancient Egypt that they were believed to possess magical powers. Cat statues were placed outside homes to ward off evil spirits, and mummified cats were included in royal tombs to accompany their owners into the afterlife.

Today, few people believe that cats have supernatural powers, but most pet owners feel a magical bond with their pets, whether they are dogs, cats, hamsters, rabbits, horses, or parrots. The lives of pets and their people become inextricably intertwined, providing strong emotional and physical rewards for both humans and animals. People of all ages can benefit from the loving companionship of a pet. Not surprisingly, then, pet ownership is widespread. Recent statistics indicate that about 60 percent of all households in the United States and Canada have at least one pet, while the figure is close to 50 percent of households in the United Kingdom. For millions of people, therefore, pets truly have become their "best friends."

Finding the best animal friend can be a challenge, however. Not only are there many types of domesticated pets, but each has specific needs, characteristics, and personality traits. Even within a category of pets, such as dogs, different breeds will flourish in different surroundings and with different treatment. For example, a German Shepherd may not be the right pet for a person living in a cramped urban apartment; that person might be better off caring for a smaller dog like a Toy Poodle or Shih Tzu, or perhaps a cat. On the other hand, an active person who loves the outdoors may prefer the companion-

ship of a Labrador Retriever to that of a small dog or a passive indoor pet like a goldfish or hamster.

The joys of pet ownership come with certain responsibilities. Bringing a pet into your home and your neighborhood obligates you to care for and train the pet properly. For example, a dog must be housebroken, taught to obey your commands, and trained to behave appropriately when he encounters other people or animals. Owners must also be mindful of their pet's particular nutritional and medical needs.

The purpose of the OUR BEST FRIENDS series is to provide a helpful and comprehensive introduction to pet ownership. Each book contains the basic information a prospective pet owner needs in order to choose the right pet for his or her situation and to care for that pet throughout the pet's lifetime. Training, socialization, proper nutrition, potential medical issues, and the legal responsibilities of pet ownership are thoroughly explained and discussed, and an abundance of expert tips and suggestions are offered. Whether it is a hamster, corn snake, guinea pig, or Labrador Retriever, the books in the OUR BEST FRIENDS series provide everything the reader needs to know about how to have a happy, well-adjusted, and well-behaved pet.

The small and energetic Miniature Schnauzer is among the most popular dog breeds. Miniature Schnauzers make great pets because they are friendly, intelligent, and eager to please their owners.

CHAPTER ONE

Is a Miniature Schnauzer Right for You?

It's easy to fall in love with a Miniature Schnauzer at first sight. He is a handsome little dog with enough verve and substance to please a man, enough style and practicality to please a woman, and enough playful spirit to elicit the adoration of children. He is classy, yet scrappy. He is dignified, yet down-to-earth. How can anyone not adore those cute eyebrows and distinguished beard?

There's no disputing that the Miniature Schnauzer possesses more than his fair share of charisma, but how do you know if he's "the one"? Does the Miniature Schnauzer have what it takes to become that once-in-a-lifetime dog of your dreams? Can

he fulfill the purposes you have in mind for him? And most important, can you fulfill the unique needs of a Miniature Schnauzer?

SIZE

The Miniature Schnauzer is small without being diminutive. While he can make a nice traveling companion or provide comfortable couch company, he is by no means delicate or frail. He makes an excellent choice for active owners who like to include their dogs in their adventures. The Miniature Schnauzer is also a great dog for families with children.

According to the American Kennel Club (AKC) breed standard, the Miniature Schnauzer should be

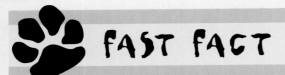

Dog owners must be prepared to make a long-term commitment before acquiring a Miniature Schnauzer. The typical Miniature Schnauzer has a life expectancy of 14 to 16 years.

between 12 and 14 inches (30.5 to 35.5 centimeters) high at the shoulder. Show dogs that fall outside of this range are disqualified, as size is a very important breed characteristic.

The breed standard also mentions the absence of "toyishness." The Miniature Schnauzer is strong-boned and sturdy. Most Miniature Schnauzers fall between 14 and 18 pounds (6 to 8 kilograms), so don't expect to carry one around in a tote bag. This gritty canine would rather walk on its own four feet than be carried, anyhow.

STRUCTURE

The Miniature Schnauzer is built squarely and solidly. Like a well-made oak chair, there is no wobble or weakness in his proportions. He enjoys incredible balance and strength for his size. With plenty of muscle and body thickness, he has an impressive countenance for a small dog.

Do you enjoy an active lifestyle? Are you interested in pursuing one of the many canine sports? Or do you simply enjoy taking long, leisurely walks? If so, the Miniature Schnauzer has the right physical endowments to meet your needs. He is an athletic and robust dog.

COAT

The Miniature Schnauzer is considered a non-shedding breed. This doesn't mean that a Miniature Schnauzer never sheds—all dogs, like all people, are constantly replacing some of their hair. But the Miniature Schnauzer sheds very little. This makes the breed a great choice for people who are allergic to other dogs, or people who simply want an exceptionally clean housemate.

But these benefits do have a price—the cost of grooming. Whether you invest in the tools to groom your dog yourself or use the services of a professional groomer, keeping a Miniature Schnauzer's coat in top condition requires time

The Miniature Schnauzer has a double coat of fur: a wiry topcoat and a soft undercoat.

and money. Schnauzers are not born with that delightfully dapper "hairdo."

Without regular brushing, the Miniature Schnauzer's profuse leg and underside furnishings can become horribly matted. While pet Schnauzers are still relatively easy to maintain if their hair is kept trimmed, show dogs require extremely high maintenance grooming in the form of hand-stripping.

COLOR

As marvelous as it is, the Miniature Schnauzer's coat doesn't offer a lot of color patterns from which to choose. The AKC and the Kennel Club (KC) in Britain recognize only three colorations of Miniature Schnauzer: salt and pepper, black and silver, and solid black. Of these, the salt and pepper is the most popular. The salt and pepper coat consists of a topcoat with hairs that have alternating bands of white and black color. These hairs are interspersed with solid black and solid white hairs, giving the coat a peppered appearance. This color is accentuated with lighter shades of gray or silver-white inside the ears and on the eyebrows, face, throat, chest, and legs, as well as under the tail. The black and silver Miniature Schnauzer has a similar color pattern, but the

The salt and pepper coat is most common among purebred Miniature Schnauzers.

contrast between the darker and lighter portions of the coat is much more pronounced. The solid black, of course, offers no contrast at all but has a rich appearance.

The reason for the limited spectrum of color in the Miniature Schnauzer is the desire of breeders to preserve the colors that have historically defined the breed. The common

If you're looking for a show dog, avoid Miniature Schnauzers with white coats. White Miniature Schnauzers are not considered good representatives of the breed, and won't be allowed to compete in AKC conformation events. However, coat color has no effect on a dog's other characteristics, such as temperament, so a white Miniature Schnauzer might make an acceptable pet.

salt and pepper coloration is shared with the Standard Schnauzer, from which the Miniature Schnauzer came. A Schnauzer with spots, stripes, or patches would hardly be recognizable as a Schnauzer. Therefore, white Schnauzers and Schnauzers with more than a small white patch on the chest are disqualified from the show ring.

CROPPING AND DOCKING

Two other characteristics that historically define this breed are its docked

tail and cropped ears. The purpose of altering the Miniature Schnauzer's appearance in these ways was to give the dog a sharper, fearless image. The Miniature Schnauzer's tail is customarily docked at the third vertebrae, and its ears are cropped and set in an alert, upright position.

Docking will be done well before you get your puppy, as it is normally performed when a puppy is only a few days old. Cropping may or may not be done by the time you acquire your Miniature Schnauzer puppy. If the ears have not been cropped, you'll need to decide whether to have this procedure done.

Keep in mind that cropping is purely a cosmetic operation that provides no health benefits for your dog. Uncropped pet dogs have become quite common, so you don't need to worry about your Miniature Schnauzer being unrecognizable as a purebred if he has natural ears. However, uncropped dogs are often at a disadvantage in the show ring. Before you decide to have this procedure done, be sure to review all the pros and cons (see Chapter 6 for more information).

INTELLIGENCE AND COMPANIONABILITY

The Miniature Schnauzer obviously has many fine physical attributes. Its temperament offers much to admire as well. These small dogs have big attitudes, a terrier-like trait that has facilitated their placement in the AKC terrier group. According to their AKC breed standard, Miniature Schnauzers are spirited, yet obedient. They are bold, yet not overly aggressive.

The Miniature Schnauzer is also an exceptionally intelligent dog. This, combined with the breed's obedient nature, makes training relatively easy. With a little bit of work, you can have a truly wonderful canine companion.

Does the Miniature Schnauzer's temperament sound too good to be true? Somewhere along the line, a bit of spunk was thrown into this breed's ancestry. While some might consider the breed's independent streak to be a form of stubbornness, Miniature Schnauzer lovers recognize the value of a spirited, game personality. Life with a Miniature Schnauzer is definitely not boring.

Miniature Schnauzers with solid black coats have a striking appearance.

The key to enjoying a Miniature Schnauzer's perky but sometimes testy personality is to redirect and channel his energy in positive directions. You don't need to quash his spirit. You just need to show him what to do with it. With firm leadership and guidance on your part, a Miniature Schnauzer will become a fun, affectionate, and faithful companion.

WATCHDOGS

The Miniature Schnauzer's plucky disposition is rooted in instincts that have been strengthened through many years of selective breeding. Another trait deeply entrenched in the Miniature Schnauzer's psyche is a desire to alert you to anything that seems amiss. The Miniature Schnauzer takes his duties as a watchdog very seriously.

This means that Miniature Schnauzers like to bark. Some bark *a lot*. While there are definite advantages to having your own personal alarm system, excessive barking can be quite irritating. You'll need to teach your dog to bark only when appropriate.

ENERGY LEVEL

Like other dogs in the terrier group, the Miniature Schnauzer has a good supply of energy. When not engaged in the serious job of being a watchdog, Miniature Schnauzers are happy, playful canines that love to frolic with you. But they're just as content to spend time lap lounging or couch cuddling.

HEALTH CARE COSTS

The cost of canine companionship goes well beyond the purchase price or adoption fee. The most expensive ongoing costs you will face are related to health care. Contact veterinary hospitals in your area to determine costs for the following:

Physical exam
Office charge
Vaccinations
Fecal tests
Worming medications

Heartworm test
Heartworm medication
Neuter or spay surgery
Cropping surgery

In this sense, their need for exercise isn't insatiable, though they do enjoy a good game of fetch and a brisk walk once a day. A moderately high energy level makes the Miniature Schnauzer a practical, fun pet for many lifestyles.

PREY DRIVE

One of the ways the Miniature Schnauzer enjoys expending its energy is in the chase. These high-spirited dogs inherited a substantial prey drive from both their herding ancestors and their ratting ancestors. The prey drive is what inspires a herding dog to chase and direct cattle or sheep. It is also the driving force behind a terrier's almost obsessive pursuit of small animals.

You can expect your Miniature Schnauzer to find great joy in the pursuit of squirrels and other rodents. While this strong instinct may also fuel the Miniature Schnauzer's enthusiasm for play, it may necessitate keeping your dog on

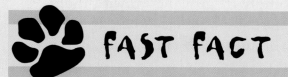

FAST FACT

You don't need a big dog to prevent home burglaries; you just need a barking alarm. The Miniature Schnauzer can fulfill this duty with gusto.

QUICK FACTS

Miniature Schnauzer facts-at-a-glance:

Does well with city living.........................Yes
Does well with suburban living ....Yes
Does well with country living.................Yes
Gets along with children ....Yes
Gets along with cats....................Sometimes
Gets along with dogs ....Yes
Gets along with small pets ....No
Exercise requirements ....Moderately high

a leash or in a fenced yard when outside. It may also affect the dog's relationship to other pets.

MINIATURE SCHNAUZERS AND OTHER PETS

Keep in mind that while prey drive can be controlled, you cannot get rid of it completely. The behavior is hardwired in a dog. If you already keep rodents or rabbits in your house as pets, it might not be a good idea to get a Miniature Schnauzer. The Miniature Schnauzer is not always the best match for households with cats, either.

If you are adopting an adult Miniature Schnauzer, consider testing his reaction to other animals before bringing him home. Or take

A Miniature Schnauzer can get along with another dog in your household. This is particularly true if that dog is about the same size as your Schnauzer, like the West Highland White Terrier (above, right). Two dogs are more likely to become friends if they are different genders; in that case, spaying and/or neutering will eliminate the risk of unwanted puppies.

the dog on a trial basis. In many cases pets of different species can establish their own "agreements" and live in harmony. Some Miniature Schnauzers, however, are simply not capable of subduing their powerful instincts.

Although puppies often learn to get along with other animal species simply by growing up with them, there are no guarantees. If you get a Miniature Schnauzer pup, he may always enjoy chasing your cat. While this is just an expression of the dog's natural prey drive instinct, chances are the cat won't be amused. Another dog, however, often makes a wonderful Schnauzer playmate.

MINIATURE SCHNAUZERS AND CHILDREN

Many years ago in Germany, the Miniature Schnauzer earned the job of *Kinderwachter* ("child watcher"). Kids seem to satisfy two needs for this breed—the need for fun, and the need for a serious job. Miniature Schnauzers appreciate the lively excitement that children provide, and they naturally assume the responsibility of keeping watch over kids.

At the same time, the Miniature Schnauzer's size is perfect for children. These dogs won't knock a small child down with a mere wag of the tail. Yet they aren't as fragile as other small dogs. All things considered, the Miniature Schnauzer makes an ideal family dog.

A VERSATILE COMPANION

The Miniature Schnauzer is comfortable in the city, the suburbs, or the country. Miniature Schnauzers can adapt to living in an apartment, a home with a yard, or an expansive country estate. No matter where you live, however, your Miniature Schnauzer will want to be at your side constantly. Do you like sailing? Don't forget to take your Miniature Schnauzer with you. Do you like bicycling? Better get a pet seat or bike trailer to take along your little friend.

Such outings are more than just chances for you and your little buddy to have some fun together. They also provide opportunities for you to socialize your Miniature Schnauzer. A Miniature Schnauzer that is kept isolated from the outside world may develop an unreasonable suspicion of strangers. This could result in inappropriate territorial aggression—your dog's guarding instinct taken to an undesirable extreme. So socialization is extremely important for Miniature Schnauzers.

However, getting your dog out and about doesn't mean you should ever keep a Miniature Schnauzer as an outdoor pet. Your Miniature Schnauzer thrives on your attention. He likes to make you laugh. He likes to impress you with his bravado. He likes to amaze you with his genius. And he likes to infect you with his zest for life. He wants to be with you both indoors and out.

The Miniature Schnauzer is an amazingly versatile companion. He can make a docile pet for the elderly, a sporting companion for the young at heart, or an all-purpose family dog. The Miniature Schnauzer has a lot to offer anyone who is willing to meet his needs for exercise, grooming, and training. If you are such a person, prepare to let your heart become captivated by this incredible canine!

CHAPTER TWO

Finding the Right Miniature Schnauzer

All members of a particular canine breed share certain physical characteristics and behavioral traits. But, like people, every dog is an individual. When deciding which Miniature Schnauzer is right for you, remember that temperament is affected by factors such as breeding quality, sex, age, and previous experiences.

Of course, before you bring any Miniature Schnauzer into your home, you'll want to understand a bit about what makes the breed tick. For this, it's necessary to look into the past.

THE HISTORY OF PUREBRED DOGS

Before the mid-1800s, dogs were not distinguished by breed, but rather by

An adorable Miniature Schnauzer might be the right dog for you.

type. While type included general appearance—such as long hair versus short hair, or large size versus small size—the physical characteristics of dogs had not yet been refined enough so that individual breeds could be clearly recognized.

Dogs were also categorized according to the function they served. Some dogs were valued for their companionship qualities. Others were valued for their talents in hunting, herding, or guarding. The Schnauzer, which was originally a medium-sized dog, was prized for its guarding and herding abilities, as well as its skill in vermin eradication. This type of dog originated in Germany, where it may have been known as far back as the Middle Ages. The name comes from the German word *Schnauze*, which refers to the dog's bearded snout. Although breed standards to define the Schnauzer's size, construction, and color weren't developed until 1880, the Schnauzer-type dog was already distinguished by its wiry topcoat, which differentiated it from other working farm dogs.

It was this medium-sized dog (now known as the Standard Schnauzer) that gave rise to both the Giant Schnauzer and the Miniature Schnauzer. These different size varieties were developed to meet partic-

ular needs. The Giant Schnauzer was bred to drive cattle, while the Miniature Schnauzer was bred to serve as a ratter, companion, and economical farm dog.

THE MINIATURE SCHNAUZER IN GERMANY

In order to create a smaller version of the Schnauzer dog, the genes of smaller dog types had to be infused.

Schnauzers come in three sizes: miniature, which are about 12 inches (30 cm) tall at the shoulder; standard, which are about 18 inches (46 cm) at the shoulder; and giant (pictured), which stand about 24 inches (60 cm) at the shoulder.

Small pinschers, which were common in Germany, were likely candidates.

These dogs had terrier-like personalities and often sported docked tails and cropped ears. The Affenpinscher and the Miniature Pinscher both predate the Miniature Schnauzer, a breed both probably influenced. Besides contributing a smaller size, they have a game attitude and ratting abilities that are obviously present in the Miniature Schnauzer. (*Pinscher* is a German word that refers to the bite these dogs use to dispatch their quarry.)

Unlike English terriers, Germany's pinschers were not bred specifically to "go to ground," which involves pursuing vermin into their burrows. However, their drive to pursue and dispatch rodents was just as strong. This could explain some of the temperamental differences between Miniature Schnauzers and

FAST FACT

Miniature Schnauzers were often called *Zwergschnauzers* in their native Germany. *Zwerg* means "dwarf."

other members of the terrier group. While exhibiting the drive and independent nature of a terrier, the Miniature Schnauzer does not possess the terrier's wanderlust. His obedience and loyalty to his owner is strong, and his protective instinct is well developed. This unusual combination of traits is perhaps what inspired early breeders to create the Miniature Schnauzer.

As breeders developed a small version of Schnauzer, a number of untraditional colors were produced. Black and salt and pepper were already known in the Standard Schnauzer, but black and tan (a common pinscher coloration) and yellow appeared in the Miniature Schnauzer. Careful breeding eventually eliminated these aberrations and returned the Miniature Schnauzer to the historically monochrome colors of its larger namesake.

The black German Poodle is often credited with helping to stabilize the color of the Miniature Schnauzer, but this breed's genetic

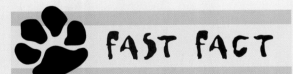

FAST FACT

The Miniature Schnauzer, while possessing many traits similar to terriers, has little if any true terrier blood in its lineage. Most terriers originated in the British Isles. The Miniature Schnauzer hails from Germany.

Dogs like the Keeshond (top left), Pomeranian (top right), and Miniature Pinscher (bottom) each contributed characteristics to the Miniature Schnauzer breed.

influence would have been minimal. Although poodles were popular in Germany, their prepotency for curly hair would have been a serious obstacle in preserving the Schnauzer's rough coat.

The Miniature Schnauzer's development is also attributed to crosses with Spitz-type dogs. The Wolfsspitz, later called the Keeshond, and the Pomeranian would have been desirable contributors. These wolf-like dogs possessed double coats with salt and pepper coloration, and they had strong guarding and herding backgrounds.

Early versions of the Miniature Schnauzer were called Wirehaired

Miniature Pinschers. They were reportedly exhibited in dog shows under this name as early as 1899. However, the lineage of Wirehaired Miniature Pinschers was not recorded until 1902, when the German Pinscher Klub issued the first *Pinscher-Zuchtbuch* (Pinscher Studbook). The breed became known as Miniature Schnauzers after the German Pinscher Klub consolidated with the Bavarian Schnauzer Klub to form the German Pinscher-Schnauzer Klub in 1918.

THE MINIATURE SCHNAUZER IN THE UNITED STATES

Miniature Schnauzers were first imported into the United States in 1923. American fanciers were a few years behind their European counterparts, however, calling their first Schnauzer breed club the Wirehaired Pinscher Club of America. This club, formed in 1925, represented both Standard and Miniature Schnauzers. It wasn't until 1933, after this organization split into separate clubs for Standards and Miniatures, that the smaller members of this breed were finally called Schnauzers.

When the AKC first recognized Wirehaired Pinschers as a breed in 1926, both the Standard and Miniature varieties were placed in the terrier group. After much peti-

Piney was a Miniature Schnauzer owned by President Herbert Hoover in the 1920s.

tioning, the Standard Schnauzer was moved into the working group in 1945, in recognition of its true purpose as a working farm dog. The Miniature Schnauzer, however, remains in the terrier group with breeds that have little in common with it genetically but that share similarities in temperament and purpose. It's interesting to note that the United States and Canada are the only countries where Miniature Schnauzers are classified as terriers. In most countries Miniature Schnauzers are placed in a "utility" category.

The Miniature Schnauzer's desirable size and coat qualities, along with its wonderful disposition, have contributed to its steady rise in popularity in the United States. In 2008 the Miniature Schnauzer was the AKC's 11th most registered dog breed.

BREED STANDARDS AND CONFORMATION

Today's Miniature Schnauzer has found a secure place in the homes and hearts of dog lovers. This remarkable canine is the product of decades of selective breeding by dedicated fanciers. Those breeding efforts might have failed miserably if not for a shared vision.

Producing a recognizable purebred dog requires a breeding program that consistently passes key traits—both physical and temperamental—from one generation to the next. One advantage of purebred dogs is predictability. When you get

Reputable breeders of Miniature Schnauzers strive to produce dogs that adhere closely to the Standard of Perfection.

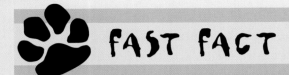

a purebred dog, you basically know how that dog will look and act when grown. But in order to maintain uniformity in a breed, breeders all have to be on the same page.

Breed standards were created to provide guidelines for breeders. They consist of detailed descriptions that include size, color, structure, and temperament—all the traits that breeders should strive to replicate in their dogs. While nature rarely allows us to achieve the level of perfection represented in a breed standard, the standard ensures that serious Miniature Schnauzer breeders all aim for the same ideal.

WHERE TO FIND A MINIATURE SCHNAUZER

Miniature Schnauzers aren't hard to find. Popular dogs, they are available through breeders, animal shelters, rescue groups, and pet shops. But which source is best? The answer to that question depends on your needs, finances, and living situation.

If you plan to show your dog, you should seek an established breeder. This is also the best source for a top-quality pet dog. You can expect to pay considerably higher prices for a high-caliber canine, but you get a lot more for the money. A reputable breeder puts considerable effort into health testing her stock and socializing her puppies. Because of this, she may offer health and temperament guarantees for her puppies.

Reputable breeders are very committed to their animals and can be very particular about who is allowed to take one of their puppies home. You can expect to sign a purchase contract that will outline your responsibilities in caring for the puppy you purchase.

The best place to meet serious fanciers of the Miniature Schnauzer is at local dog shows. A list of breeders and local breed clubs is available on the Web site of the American Miniature Schnauzer Club (http://amsc.us/).

In addition to professional breeders, there are "backyard" breeders who offer Miniature Schnauzer puppies. You can find these hobbyists through classified ads. In most cases, backyard breeders truly like dogs. But they may or may not have much knowledge about genetics or good breeding practices. Although you're unlikely to find a future champion from this type of breeder, you will find more reasonable prices.

Regardless of which type of breeder you choose, you should evaluate a puppy and its environment in person. Can you see at least one of the parent dogs to get an indication of what the puppy will be like as an adult? Are the puppies kept in a clean environment? Do they appear healthy and well socialized? Most important, does the breeder have the puppy's paperwork in order?

By the time a puppy is ready for sale, he should have received one set of vaccinations and a worming. Can the breeder provide documentation of this? Are the puppy's registration papers available? If you choose a breeder judiciously, she may become more than just a source for a healthy Miniature Schnauzer puppy. She may also become your adviser, mentor, and friend.

Animal shelters and rescue groups are great sources for affordable purebred dogs. Check Petfinder.com or the Web site of the American Miniature Schnauzer Club for rescue groups that specialize in the Miniature Schnauzer. An animal

QUESTIONS TO ASK A BREEDER

Regarding health:
- Does the puppy have at least one set of vaccinations and a worming?
- Can you provide documentation of vaccinations and wormings?
- Have the parent dogs been tested for any hereditary health conditions?

Regarding socialization:
- How old is the puppy? *Puppies should stay with their mother until eight weeks of age.*

- Has the puppy been allowed outside?
- Has the puppy received daily handling from people?

Regarding purebred quality:
- Do you have AKC registration papers available?
- Do you have pedigree (family tree) records available?
- Can I see the parent dog(s)?
- Do any of the puppy's ancestors have conformation titles?

shelter or rescue group is a good choice if you prefer to bypass the puppy stage and get an adult Miniature Schnauzer. Best of all, adopted dogs bring a sense of satisfaction you can only get by choosing to love a homeless animal.

These benefits do not come without some disadvantages, however. Such dogs often have behavior issues. Fortunately, most problem behaviors are easily solved with training. In fact, an adopted adult dog often takes less time and effort to train than a puppy. But you should recognize your limitations and avoid choosing a dog that has serious issues you don't feel qualified to handle.

You should think twice before purchasing a Miniature Schnauzer pup from a flea market, pet store, online site, or similar source. Buying a purebred puppy from a source that does not allow you to inspect the environment in which the puppy was raised or see one of the puppy's parents is risky business. Are you willing to endure the stress, heartache, and expense of owning a dog that has serious health and behavioral problems?

Some pet shops offer health guarantees, but these are almost worth-

BUYING FROM A PET STORE

A pet store may not be the best place to purchase a Miniature Schnauzer. Unlike responsible breeders, pet stores are in business for profit. Many of the dogs they sell come from puppy mills—kennels that breed large numbers of dogs under terrible conditions. In these settings, dogs are very rarely bred responsibly, and they are almost never given adequate love or medical attention. Females are usually bred every heat cycle until they can no longer carry puppies to term.

Very few of the puppies that come from these mills have been socialized properly. As a result, the puppies often have behavioral problems that make them difficult to train. Poor physical conditions are also common. Miniature Schnauzers bred in puppy mills are frequently underfed, riddled with parasites, and infected with kennel cough.

If you do decide to buy from a pet store, do your research first. There are some good pet stores, but they are few and far between. Buying an unhealthy Schnauzer now can lead to heartbreak later. Furthermore, you wouldn't want to reward the inhumane treatment of animals.

less. Most pet-shop puppies come from puppy mills, where profit is the only consideration. In these awful settings, mother dogs are bred as often as possible, until their health is utterly ruined. Even if that "puppy in the window" seems awfully cute, a true dog lover won't want to contribute to the suffering puppy mills create.

Online sources that promise to ship puppies anywhere in the country present their own problems. First, shipping can be very stressful, and sometimes deadly, for young puppies. And second, it can be difficult to deal with a breeder located out of state. What if you aren't satisfied with your purchase? The best rule is this: Never buy a puppy sight-unseen.

CHOOSING YOUR MINIATURE SCHNAUZER

"Choose your friends wisely" is sound advice, whether the friends in question are of the two- or four-legged variety. Take a moment to think about what you consider an ideal canine companion. Don't forget to consider gender, age, purpose, temperament, and health to determine if a particular puppy or dog fits your mental picture of the perfect pooch.

MALE OR FEMALE: When it comes to Miniature Schnauzers, gender has

Before choosing a pet, think about the characteristics and temperament that you would like your dog to possess. Knowing exactly what you want will help you pick the Miniature Schnauzer that best fits your needs.

little effect on temperament. Males and females of the breed both have a sweet, obedient nature. Unless you're considering showing or breeding your Miniature Schnauzer, it shouldn't matter whether you choose a male or a female, provided you neuter a male or spay a female.

If you've never shown or bred Miniature Schnauzers, be aware that these pursuits can be expensive and time-consuming. Before you leap in, do your homework. There is much to know. Also try to find an experienced mentor who can provide trustworthy advice and guidance.

PUPPY OR ADULT: There are many reasons to choose a puppy. They're fun, they're cute, and you can have complete control over how they're raised. There are also many reasons not to choose a puppy. They're expensive, they're undisciplined, they chew on everything, and they make messes on the carpet. If you have your heart set on getting a Miniature Schnauzer puppy, recognize that

puppies require a lot of time for supervision and training. Even so, most people find that the benefits outweigh the burdens.

There are times, though, when acquiring an adult dog is the better option. If you want a mature canine that has outgrown the nonsense of youth and will fit into your busy life with a minimum of effort, an adult Miniature Schnauzer might be your dream dog. Adult dogs have greater attention spans, so they are often easier to train.

But dogs don't come in just two age groups. In your quest for a good friend, you might come across an older puppy, a young adult, or even a senior

Puppies are cute, but they're also a lot of work. Be certain that you are ready for the responsibility and time commitment required to properly train and care for a puppy.

Miniature Schnauzer. You can narrow your choices by considering the various developmental stages and what you like or don't like about them. Some people become frustrated with the testy young-adult stage (six months to two years old), while other people appreciate this as the perfect age for obedience training. Some people discount senior dogs as too old, while others adore the benefits of a mature, calmer dog. What age fits you?

SHOW OR COMPANION: Obviously, if your vision of the perfect dog includes trophies and titles, you'll need to restrict your search to dogs with the right qualities to make those goals a reality. When getting started in conformation competition, the first order of business is to purchase the best-quality puppy you can afford.

The show prospects you encounter will likely be in the "older puppy" category. Breeders often keep puppies with promise into late puppy-hood to see which ones develop the most show-worthy characteristics. Also, breeders do not part easily with their puppy prodigies. You may have to be willing to enter into a purchase contract under which the breeder retains breeding rights for your pooch.

EVALUATING TEMPERAMENT: Whether you envision your dream dog attaining stardom on the show circuit or you're simply looking for a humble house pet, there is one trait that warrants exceptional scrutiny: temperament. Trainability, sociability, and adaptability all hinge on temperament.

Forget the old idea that you should choose the boldest, most rambunctious pup in the litter. He's the one that pushes all the other pups out of the way to get to you first. He's the one that jumps all over you as if he's already chosen you to take him home. He's also the one most likely to become dominant and hard to train. Unless you are an experienced dog owner who likes the challenge of a dog with attitude, think twice about choosing this pup.

Likewise, unless you have an enormous heart and an even larger

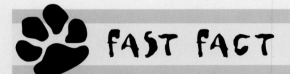

FAST FACT

In terms of obedience and working intelligence, the Miniature Schnauzer is near the top of the canine class. Of the 134 dog breeds ranked in psychologist Stanley Coren's seminal book *The Intelligence of Dogs*, the Miniature Schnauzer came in 12th.

pocketbook, you'd be well advised not to choose the pitifully shy runt of the litter. The chances are good that the puppy hiding in a corner or being picked on by littermates will grow up to be fearful or sickly.

If you want a mentally balanced, versatile, and adaptable dog, most experts recommend choosing a puppy that falls somewhere between the boldest and the shyest in a litter. A puppy that takes time to analyze a situation before acting shows intelligence. A pup that is friendly but not overbearing will be more likely to accept your leadership.

EVALUATING HEALTH: It goes without saying that you should choose a healthy Miniature Schnauzer, but do you know how to recognize one?

You should avoid any puppy that has discharge from the nose or eyes, coughing, wheezing, vomiting, or diarrhea. These are obvious signs of illness.

Watch, too, for more subtle signs of health problems. A dull coat or flaky skin may signal the presence of external parasites. A bloated, pot-bellied appearance is a good indication of intestinal worms. Squinty eyes are evidence of pain or a feeling of general malaise. Also be observant of the puppy's attitude. The Miniature Schnauzer is an exuberant breed. If a Miniature Schnauzer pup appears overly placid, this might be a sign of lethargy rather than a calm temperament.

When evaluating an adult dog, it's advisable to do a head-to-tail inspection—regardless of whether the dog has been examined by a veterinarian. This will give you a good idea of the dog's health. It will also shed light on how well the dog tolerates having his various body parts handled. Does he snap at you when you check his teeth? Does he fight like a wild animal when you try to handle his feet? Dogs that are not used to being handled may offer some resistance, but you want to steer clear of dogs that show obvious signs of aggression.

CHAPTER THREE

Responsible Pet Ownership

You and your Miniature Schnauzer will share some wonderful times. Think of all the brisk walks, all the places you'll explore together, all the snuggles you'll enjoy.

Of course, the privilege of dog ownership comes with responsibilities. By taking a Miniature Schnauzer into your home, you are accepting an obligation to care for the dog. You are also accepting a duty to other people. This means abiding by all public ordinances and regulations regarding pet ownership. It means ensuring that your dog is never a danger or even a nuisance to others. It means striving to be courteous and

Owning a Miniature Schnauzer is much like having a child. Your pet's well-being is your responsibility, and you will be held accountable for any damage he may cause.

Your Miniature Schnauzer should have a sturdy collar with an identification tag. The collar can also hold any other tags that local laws require your pet to carry, such as proof of a rabies vaccination or a local dog license. Printing the phrase "needs medication" on a dog's identification tag can encourage the prompt return of a lost pet.

respectful whenever you and your dog are out and about.

IDENTIFICATION

One of the first responsibilities you should attend to after acquiring your Miniature Schnauzer is to provide your pet with identification. In the event your dog ever becomes lost, identification will help keep him safe and facilitate his return. When most people find a lost dog, they look for an identification tag on a collar. This should be considered a mandatory form of canine ID.

Collars with identification tags are not infallible. Your dog can wriggle out of his collar, and thieves can remove it. That is why it's also a good idea to invest in a permanent form of ID. Some dog owners favor tattoos. Tattooed dogs are marked with a series of numbers—usually the tattoo registry number or the dog's AKC registration number. Common locations for identification tattoos include the belly and the inside of the thigh.

Pet owners who are uncomfortable with tattooing can instead choose microchip implantation. In this method, a computer chip that is about the size of a grain of rice is injected under the dog's skin, between the shoulders. The chip contains data about how to contact the

FAST FACT

Tattooing or microchip implantation can be performed at a local veterinary clinic.

dog's owner. Most veterinarians and animal shelters have scanners that can detect and read microchips. You can purchase a microchip from your veterinarian, or check with local animal welfare organizations to see if they offer discounted microchips.

It is not enough just to provide your dog with identification. Your Miniature Schnauzer is an especially appealing target for thieves, as purebred dogs command high prices on the pet market. You should be watchful whenever your dog is outside of your home, whether in your yard, in your vehicle, or at the dog park.

PET INSURANCE

When it comes to the health of your Miniature Schnauzer, prevention is the best policy. Unfortunately, you can't always protect your canine from the hazards of life. Your sanguine Schnauzer wouldn't be happy living in a bubble, anyway. For this reason, you might want to consider the benefits of pet insurance.

Can you imagine anything more heartbreaking than having to euthanize your best friend because you couldn't afford the veterinary expenses to treat his illness or injury? Pet insurance allows you to take the cost out of the equation when making difficult decisions regarding your dog's health.

PREVENTING PET THEFT

- **Don't** leave your dog unattended in a vehicle.
- **Don't** leave your dog unattended in your yard (even if fenced or tied out).
- **Don't** leave your dog tied outside a convenience store or other business establishment.

- **Do** provide a permanent form of ID for your dog, such as a microchip or tattoo.
- **Do** keep a current photo and description of your dog.
- **Do** report any suspicious strangers in your neighborhood to the police.

Pet insurance first became available more than 30 years ago. Hundreds of companies now provide insurance coverage for dogs, cats, and other pets.

Pet insurance operates in much the same way as health insurance for people. The pet owner pays an annual premium, the size of which depends on the insurance carrier, the level of coverage, the age of the pet, and other factors. Most pet insurance policies have a deductible, which means that the insurance carrier begins paying claims only after the pet owner has spent a certain amount of money out of pocket. Most plans also include co-payments for each visit to the veterinarian.

The scope of coverage depends on the individual insurance company and the policy. Some policies provide coverage for routine veterinary care, like annual physical exams, while others cover only major medical expenses. Of course, the more a policy covers, the higher the premium.

Is pet insurance worth the expense? Bear in mind that veterinary services have expanded rapidly in the last decade. Many of the same diagnostic and treatment options that are available to humans—such

as MRIs, CT scans, and chemotherapy—are available to pets. This is great news for your dog's health, but it can be bad news for your wallet. Buying an insurance policy for your Miniature Schnauzer may make sense. If you are interested in pursuing this option, evaluate insurers and policies carefully. Be sure to check out the exclusions. Many policies won't cover hereditary problems or preexisting conditions.

In lieu of purchasing pet insurance, you might consider regularly putting aside a sum of money to cover future veterinary expenses. The best policy is to be prepared.

CANINE POPULATION CONTROL

Protecting your own dog is a natural desire—you love your Miniature Schnauzer more than apple pie. But what can you do for other dogs? Although you might not have the time to volunteer at a local animal shelter, there is one thing you can do to benefit almost every animal welfare organization in the country: neuter or spay your pet.

Pet overpopulation has become a huge national problem. The Humane Society of the United States (HSUS) estimates that 3 million to 4 million cats and dogs are euthanized every year because there aren't enough homes for them. Responsible pet ownership requires that you prevent your dog from producing unwanted puppies.

Spayed or neutered dogs are ineligible for dog show competitions, but unless you plan to show or breed your Miniature Schnauzer, there really aren't any good reasons not to have the dog surgically sterilized. If you can't afford the $300 charged by some vets for the procedure, investigate a low-cost spay/neuter clinic. There you might pay as little as $50.

Conversely, there are many reasons to have your dog neutered or spayed. Sterilization simply makes dogs better pets. It helps to eliminate

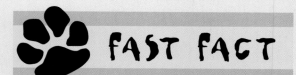

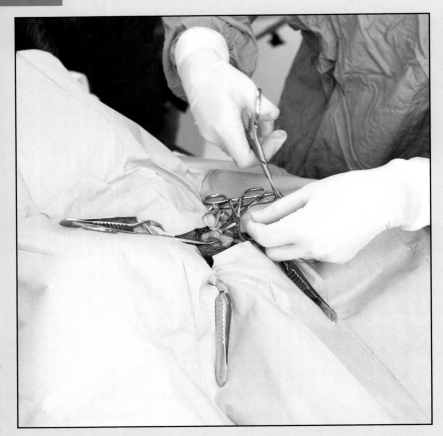

Choosing whether or not to spay or neuter your Miniature Schnauzer is an important decision. The procedure does provide certain benefits with regard to your dog's health and behavior. However, if you plan to show your Miniature Schnauzer in competitive events like conformation shows, he or she will have to remain intact.

sex-related behaviors that cause problems for dogs and their owners. In the case of male dogs, it helps subdue the urge to roam in search of mates. It also helps prevent marking, or urinating on, objects in the home. And it can help lessen aggressive tendencies.

Females that haven't been spayed go into a messy heat cycle twice per year and can easily produce unwanted litters. Repeated pregnancies take a toll on a female dog's health. Plus, a spayed female can't contract certain serious and potentially life-

threatening conditions, such as pyometra (an infected uterus).

LICENSING

Municipalities throughout the United States require people to purchase a license for each dog they own. Generally, dog licenses must be renewed annually. Failure to comply can lead to a fine.

Licensing requirements enable communities to enforce limits on the number of dogs per household. Controlling the canine population is a concern especially in urban areas, where large numbers of dogs can produce excessive noise and waste and lead to conflict among human residents. Licensing requirements also help public health authorities ensure that dogs have been vaccinated against rabies.

RABIES VACCINATION

Rabies is a serious viral disease that affects the nervous system. If untreated, it is fatal. Rabies is almost always spread through the bite of an infected animal. Pet dogs can get rabies, and they can transmit it to humans. To protect your Miniature Schnauzer—as well as yourself, your family, and your neighbors—you must make sure your dog has been vaccinated against rabies and receives periodic booster shots.

Before they will issue a dog license, municipalities require proof that the dog's rabies inoculations are up-to-date. In addition, state governments have enacted laws mandating rabies vaccinations for pet dogs. The specifics vary from state to state, but in most cases a three-year vaccine is required. Be sure to check the rabies requirements for your state.

Thanks to rabies-vaccination laws and the continued compliance of responsible pet owners, the incidence of dog-to-human rabies transmission is nearly zero.

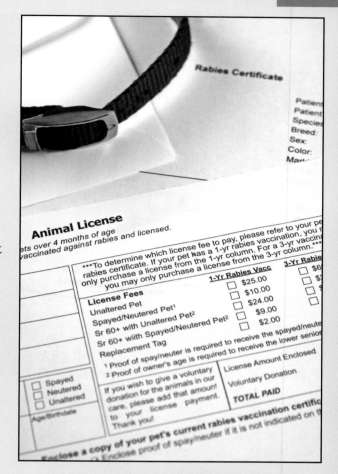

Be aware of the legal requirements related to dog ownership in your community. Pet owners who do not have their animals properly licensed and vaccinated face steep fines, and possibly even the loss of their pets.

LEASH LAWS

Almost every community has ordinances classified as "leash laws," which prohibit dog owners from allowing their dogs to run at large. Some ordinances require that dogs be confined within the owner's property or on leash when out in public;

If you plan to allow your Miniature Schnauzer the run of your yard, you'll need a sturdy fence. Pickets should be close together so your pet can't wriggle through, and the fence should extend to the ground, to discourage attempts to tunnel underneath.

others say simply that a dog must always be reasonably controlled. Violations can result in fines.

Dogs that are allowed to roam can cause all sorts of problems, from making a mess of people's garbage to causing auto accidents or biting pedestrians. However, responsible dog owners recognize that keeping a dog leashed or confined to their own property isn't just a matter of respect for other people. It also keeps the dog safe.

But how do you keep your Miniature Schnauzer on your proper-

ty? Dogs love to explore. They love to visit all the other dogs in the neighborhood. They love to chase squirrels into the next county. With training, some dogs can be taught always to stay within the territory you establish for them, but other dogs never learn this lesson. Fencing—wood, chain link, or electronic—is a good idea for keeping your Miniature Schnauzer inside your yard. If a fence isn't practical, a tie-out (tether) will work. Beware of leaving your dog tied outside unattended. Dogs can become strangled if the tie-out line gets caught on something. The best option for a tie-out is a trolley system that can be strung between two buildings or trees to give your dog a running area.

NUISANCE LAWS

Even if you keep your Miniature Schnauzer on your own property, your pooch could still annoy neighbors—and you could run afoul of nuisance laws. Many localities have ordinances prohibiting frequent or prolonged noise, or loud noise at night. A dog's excessive barking may violate such ordinances.

Miniature Schnauzers are by nature very vocal. Thus you should take extra pains to ensure that your dog doesn't create a barking nui-

sance for neighbors. It pays to address the barking issue right from the beginning. The first day you bring your Miniature Schnauzer home, you should form good "barking management" habits. Recognize when your dog barks for the right reasons—for instance, when someone rings your doorbell. Praise your dog for performing his watchdog duty well. Then expect him to cease barking. Once your dog has notified you of the interloper on your property, he has no reason to continue barking.

Make this clear to your dog by saying "quiet," then rewarding him with a treat when he stops barking. If your dog continues to carry on as if the world were coming to an end,

BEING A CONSIDERATE OWNER

- Always ask if it's OK for your dog to approach someone.
- Be diligent about cleaning up after your dog during walks, at the dog park, or while on vacation.
- Prevent your dog from barking in your absence by providing treat-dispensing toys or other distractions to keep your pup busy.

- Always keep your dog leashed, confined, or under your control.
- Teach your dog good manners so he doesn't jump on people, beg, or knock people over while rushing out the door.
- Don't allow your dog to pester guests. If he becomes annoying, remove him from the room.

you may need to use something to break his focus. You can make a "shaker can" by placing pennies or pebbles in a tin can and taping the end shut. If you throw this near—but not at—your dog, the noise will help interrupt his barking behavior.

Just as you reward your dog for appropriate barking, you should discourage him from inappropriate barking. If your dog barks every time a plane flies overhead, or carries on ridiculously when he sees a pedestrian a half mile down the street, go through the motions of checking out your dog's warning. Then act very disappointed in your dog's poor performance as a watchdog and walk away with a firm "quiet" command. If your dog doesn't respond, use the shaker can to get his attention and give him the "quiet" command again. No rewards should be forthcoming for inappropriate alerts, even if your dog quiets down when told.

If you practice these management techniques consistently from the beginning, your dog will become the

Your Miniature Schnauzer may feel it is his duty to alert you to the presence of pedestrians or vehicles near your home. However, it is up to you to make sure that he is properly trained so that his barking does not become a nuisance to neighbors.

best watchdog on the block instead of the most annoying pup on the planet. Your neighbors, too, may begin to appreciate your dog's reliable watchdog skills, as they will soon realize your dog doesn't bark without a reason.

LIABILITY

Dog ownership provides many assets—unconditional love, companionship, lots of wet kisses, and a warm body to snuggle with—but it also comes with liabilities. By law, you are responsible for everything your Miniature Schnauzer does. You would be amazed at the big trouble such a little dog can get into.

If your dog harms the neighbor's cat, bites the mail carrier, or digs up your neighbor's garden, you are responsible for the damage. In the case of personal injury, a lawsuit could require you to pay the injured party hundreds of thousands of dollars. Besides investing the time to train your dog to behave properly, it is also a good idea to carry homeowners or renters liability insurance.

Your Miniature Schnauzer may be a perfect angel, but that doesn't mean he is 100 percent predictable. Dogs behave like dogs, and sometimes that behavior falls outside of the human definition of appropriate. The best way to prevent conflicts—and potential liability—is to abide by leash laws and keep your dog under control at all times.

According to the U.S. Centers for Disease Control and Prevention, dogs bite nearly 5 million people in the United States every year. The majority of dog bites happen on the owner's property, so posting a warning sign there is a good idea.

FAST FACT

The great majority of dog bite victims are children. When children visit your home, make sure to supervise them closely around your Miniature Schnauzer. Also teach your own children how to treat your dog appropriately.

BE A GOOD NEIGHBOR

Many people will find your Miniature Schnauzer delightful and adorable. They'll approach you on the street and ask to pet him. Your coworkers may be curious and ask about him. Relatives, too, will probably show an interest in your charming new companion and enjoy the opportunity to visit him. Your Miniature Schnauzer may open up a whole new social dimension in your life.

But don't let all this attention go to your head and assume the whole world adores your little pooch. Some people are not particularly fond of dogs. Some are fearful of dogs. Some suffer allergic reactions to dogs. Always be attentive to how people react to your Miniature Schnauzer. Never allow the dog to approach anyone who seems reluctant.

Being a good neighbor is all about respect, including respect for the property of others. Even devoted dog lovers don't appreciate it when a neighbor's dog leaves "presents" on their lawn. Always clean up after your dog, no matter where you are. Keep a few extra waste bags in your purse, car, and coat pockets, so you're always prepared.

There is so much to be gained when dog owners take responsible pet ownership seriously. Most important, it helps to open doors for our canine friends, which provides more opportunities for us to enjoy canine companionship. We can make this world a better place for dog ownership, one dog at a time.

CHAPTER FOUR

The Best Possible Beginning

Getting a new Miniature Schnauzer can affect the dynamics of your entire family. It will alter the relationships among any other pets you have. It will change your routine and influence your moods. It may even color your perception of life.

Amid all the excitement of welcoming a new family member, it's easy to forget to make all the necessary arrangements. Take some time to prepare before bringing your new canine friend home.

LIVING ARRANGEMENTS

Consider where your pet will sleep, eat, play, and do his duty. Each of these arrangements will contribute to a smooth transition for your new pet.

Puppies are extremely cute, but they need careful attention to keep them out of trouble.

They will also prevent conflicts among family members, as everyone will have the same expectations and follow the same protocol.

Will your dog spend the night in your bedroom, a child's bedroom, or a separate room of his own? If your dog had a vote, he'd choose to be close to his human family members. However, choosing a separate room might be advisable, in case your dog or puppy has a particularly difficult time adjusting to his new home. Most people can't afford to give up precious sleep to the cries of a pup in transition, so don't feel guilty if you need to bed your dog down in another room until he becomes more accustomed to his new environment and routine.

Initially, you'll want to keep your Miniature Schnauzer in a crate at night to prevent accidents. After your dog has become acclimated to a regular potty schedule, you can change these arrangements if you like. Do you want to make the crate your dog's regular sleeping quarters? Do you want to provide a dog bed on the floor? Or do you want to allow your dog on the bed?

Accepting your dog as a bedmate is a very personal choice, but it is a perfectly reasonable option with a small, clean, low-shed dog like the Miniature Schnauzer. Although some experts recommend against it, allowing your dog on the bed only develops into a problem if your dog becomes territorial over the bed, in

KIDS AND CANINES

Here are some tips for getting children actively involved in dog ownership:

- Let the child help name the dog.
- Allow children to help make decisions in purchasing the dog's supplies.
- Select a dog-training class that allows children to participate along with their parents.

- Have children participate in feeding, grooming, and cleaning up after the dog, but with younger kids make sure to provide proper supervision.
- Let children help walk the dog.
- Encourage children to come up with new games to play with the dog.
- Help children teach the dog tricks.
- Let children enter their dog in a local pet show.

Before bringing your pet home, decide which rooms are OK for your Miniature Schnauzer to explore and which ones you want to prevent him from entering.

which case his bed privileges should be revoked. Otherwise, sharing body warmth and pillows can be enjoyable for both you and your snuggly buddy.

Eating should be an enjoyable activity for your dog, too. This means you should choose a place to feed your dog that is away from heavy traffic areas so your dog can eat without being disturbed. Your dog should not have to compete with other pets for food, either. Crates and door gates make excellent barriers to separate pets at feeding time.

Hopefully, your dog's arrival will be filled with fun, not feuds, as the Miniature Schnauzer's passion is to play. It's not as important to determine where your Miniature Schnauzer will be allowed to play as it is to determine where he will *not* be allowed to play. If there are areas of your home or yard that you want to be off-limits to your pet, now is the time to designate them. Only consistent enforcement of the boundaries will teach your dog to stay out of these areas.

Make sure both the exterior and interior of your home are safe for a Miniature Schnauzer. Certain common garden plants, such as azaleas and Calla lilies, are toxic to dogs. So are some varieties of ivy, fern, and evergreen shrubs and trees. The ASPCA provides a list of poisonous plants on its Web site at www.aspca.org/pet-care/poison-control/plants.

And while you're surveying your yard for potentially hazardous or sensitive areas such as gardens, flower beds, and woodpiles, go ahead and choose a potty area. Designating a specific area for your Miniature Schnauzer to use as a toilet will help tremendously in housetraining your dog. The scents will encourage your dog to use that area whenever you take him there.

DOG-PROOFING YOUR HOME

You should certainly restrict your dog's access to dangerous areas to keep him safe. But you need to do more. Homes are full of potential hazards. If you tried to make every unsafe area off-limits, your poor pooch would be relegated to his crate for the rest of his life! Dog-proofing your house can give your pet more room to roam and make both of your lives more enjoyable.

This is especially important for puppies, as they are chronic chewers and like to explore tastes and textures with their mouths. Make sure your puppy can't get at electrical cords, detergents, or other household chemicals. Miniature Schnauzer puppies are small and curious, which means they can easily become trapped behind furniture and appliances, or slip into uncovered heating ducts.

Rooms where dangerous items are present, such as toxic substances, electrical cords, or power tools, should be off-limits to your curious Miniature Schnauzer.

The best way to dog-proof your home is to get on your hands and knees and inspect the areas where your dog will be allowed to play. Your playful pup can stay occupied and safe in a contained area that has a clean floor with nothing but doggy toys on it. Regardless of how thoroughly you inspect his play areas, though, nothing can replace adequate supervision.

Always keep a close eye on your puppy. Puppies manage to find trouble in unbelievable ways. Adult dogs, too, should be observed closely for the first few weeks to see what types of inappropriate items attract them. If your dog seems to think rattan furniture is for chewing, use deterrents or confinement to prevent him from making this a habit. If your dog loves to sneak behind the TV to play with electrical cords, block the area off with cardboard or door gates. You'll have to find an inaccessible spot to keep your garbage, as dogs are notorious scavengers. Shoes, children's toys, and anything else you don't want destroyed should be put away until you determine what kind of fetishes your particular dog has.

HOUSEHOLD RULES AND RESPONSIBILITIES

When you establish rules in advance, such as where your dog will be allowed to go and which areas will be off-limits, everyone in the household can be consistent in enforcing those rules. But rules don't just apply to your dog.

If there are children in your home, you may have to consider setting limits for doggy playtime so your Miniature Schnauzer doesn't become

Decide who will be responsible for walking, feeding, and other care duties before bringing a Miniature Schnauzer into your home.

overstimulated or exhausted. Like people, dogs can get cranky when they're tired. Make sure your pet has plenty of downtime to recuperate. As much as your Miniature Schnauzer loves to play, he also appreciates having a quiet area, such as a crate or dog bed, where he can retreat.

Children also need to be taught how to treat their new canine family member. Children under the age of six aren't always aware that their actions can hurt an animal. Touching or pulling on ears, tail, or limbs should be strictly forbidden, regardless of how tolerant your Miniature Schnauzer may be. An adult should always be present when young children and dogs are together.

Even with limits in place, there are plenty of opportunities for children to enjoy their charming new friend. Most children love helping to care for a dog, and there is nothing wrong with distributing the canine-care duties among household members. This will help encourage your dog to develop close relationships with everyone in the family. Duties must be age-appropriate for children, of course, and you'll have to make sure children follow through with their responsibilities. Your dog should not have to suffer neglect because children lost interest in caring for him.

Although the novelty of a new dog inevitably wears off, there are ways to keep children motivated to care for their pet. First, keep it fun. Cleaning up the yard can become a search game—who can find the most? Walking your dog can be a great family activity; you can play "I spy" along the way. Create new sports when exercising your dog. How about "extreme fetch"?

Second, make dog care rewarding for your child. Show your child how much your dog loves to be brushed. Point out your dog's excitement at feeding time. And remind your child how much your dog loves him or her for doing all these things. You'll be doing more than teaching your child how to be responsible. You'll be encouraging a unique child-dog relationship that will benefit your child for a lifetime.

SUPPLIES

Dogs do not come with accessories included. Getting the necessary supplies before bringing home your Miniature Schnauzer will minimize the stress of the occasion and give you and your pup more time to play and bond.

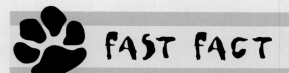

FAST FACT

Toys that are perfectly safe for one dog may pose a serious hazard for another. Always observe your dog with a new toy to make sure he plays with it appropriately. Some dogs like to pull the squeakers out of stuffed toys, which can present a choking hazard. Some dogs tend to chew up soft rubber toys and consume the parts, which can cause intestinal blockages. Promptly remove any damaged toys.

Some people enjoy dressing their Miniature Schnauzers in fun outfits.

ing. But there are a few practical tips you might want to consider.

Puppies grow quickly. Keeping your puppy's future size in mind when you buy certain items will save money. You can purchase a crate, a dog bed, and food and water bowls that are large enough to fit your pup when he is an adult. An adult-sized dog crate can always be sectioned off to make it smaller and cozier for your little guy. If you buy doggy sweaters for your Miniature Schnauzer puppy—a necessity for small dogs living in colder climates—choose stretchy fabric. That way the sweaters will fit your puppy longer.

Also, consider ease of use and maintenance. Washable items are easier to keep clean. Poop scoopers with long handles are great back-savers.

You'll need quite a few items to care for your dog, including a collar, a leash, puppy or dog food, food and water bowls, grooming supplies, a crate, a dog bed, toys, and a poop scooper. Shopping for your new pet should be fun, not a chore. For the most part, you can choose whichever designs or styles you find appeal-

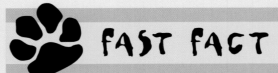

FAST FACT

A crate needs to be large enough for your Miniature Schnauzer to stand up, turn around, and lie down in comfortably. It needs to be small enough to discourage your dog from using a corner to do his duty. If you purchase an adult-size crate for a puppy, section off a portion until your puppy grows larger. Many crates are now sold with adjustable partitions for this purpose.

WHAT TO EXPECT THE FIRST FEW NIGHTS

When your puppy finally comes home, it will be such an exciting time. You'll be ecstatic. Your puppy will be bursting with curiosity about his new environment. But this exhilaration is precisely the reason you need to keep your dog's first days at home as low key as possible. All the excitement is physically and emotionally exhausting. It's stressful.

Stress contributes to illness, and it's not uncommon for puppies to suffer bouts of diarrhea or other symptoms shortly after arriving at their new homes. It's unrealistic to think you'll be able to keep your precious pup a complete secret from curious neighbors, friends, and relatives, so go ahead and have some fun showing off your captivating little canine. But try to maintain reasonable limits. Spurts of activity should be alternated with long periods of quiet and rest.

Regardless of how well you prepare for your new dog and how hard you try to minimize stress, there is no avoiding the fact that adjustments are difficult. A newly adopted adult dog may show signs of separation anxiety—including barking, howling, and chewing things up in your absence—the first couple weeks. Puppies may cry at night, lonely for their mothers and littermates. Be patient. Just when you think you can't live with it anymore, you'll notice these behaviors gradually diminishing.

Your Miniature Schnauzer will appreciate having a comfortable bed and fun toys to play with.

FAST FACT

It's not physically or mentally healthy for your dog or puppy to be confined to a crate for many hours during the day. If you work full time, consider confining your dog to a small, safe room or exercise pen.

Providing plenty of quiet time is only one way you can help your dog through this challenging period. Be sure your dog has lots of toys, which are great canine stress relievers. You can also help your Miniature Schnauzer adjust by keeping him on a strict schedule. Make sure your dog or puppy gets a good exercise session, a potty break, and a light snack before bedtime. This will encourage him to sleep. A puppy may welcome a warm water bottle wrapped in a towel as a comforting item to cuddle at night.

INTRODUCING OTHER PETS

Stress doesn't just affect your new pup. Everyone in your household will be adjusting to a new living situation, including your other pets. Sometimes pets hit it off from the very first day and become fast friends. Other times, it takes pets a while before they decide they like

each other. On occasion, however, pets never become friends—and they may or may not even learn to tolerate each other.

A proper introduction can go a long way toward fostering good relations among your pets, because first impressions mean a lot to animals. Dogs should be introduced on neutral territory, and both dogs should be on leashes for control. After they've had a chance to sniff each other, and if neither shows any animosity, take them for a walk together. A brisk pace will prevent them from becoming too focused on each other. Gradually allow the dogs to have more contact. When you see one dog offer the other a play-bow gesture, you'll know they've become friends.

Introducing your Miniature Schnauzer to a cat is also a gradual process. In this case, use door gates to separate your pets. Your cat and dog can see and sniff each other through the gates without coming in direct contact. Watch your Schnauzer carefully to see how he reacts to the feline. Does he appear obsessed with trying to chase the cat? Also pay attention to the reactions of your cat. Cats that tend to run away from dogs rather than stand up to them are more likely to incite a dog's prey drive.

In general, smaller pets like Guinea Pigs, Rabbits, Gerbils, and Hamsters will be safest if not permitted direct contact with your Miniature Schnauzer. These dogs typically have a strong drive to hunt and kill small mammals, and they won't be able to distinguish between an unwanted rodent and a beloved pet.

Some Miniature Schnauzers show little interest in chasing cats, while others think cat chasing should be a new dog sport. If your Miniature Schnauzer is in the latter group, a harmonious relationship between your pets is not meant to be.

Miniature Schnauzers, being bred to eradicate vermin, should never be expected to bond with critters of the smaller species. Keep your smaller pets safe in their cages. Larger rabbits, however, may be intimidating enough to hold their own in the company of a Schnauzer. Again, test your rabbit's and your Miniature Schnauzer's reactions to each other through door gates before allowing any direct contact.

When your Miniature Schnauzer is still a puppy, he should be introduced to at least three to five new friendly people and animals each week. Make sure that all encounters are safe and non-threatening.

COGNITIVE AND SOCIAL DEVELOPMENT

All your preparations help to ensure a great start to your new life with a very special dog. But there is one more thing you should think about when planning the best possible beginning for your Miniature Schnauzer: his cognitive and social development. Puppies and young dogs go through developmental phases that have profound effects on their future temperaments. Do you want a dog that is friendly with your guests or suspicious of them? Do you want a dog that gets along with other dogs or is aggressive toward them? Do you want a dog that is confident in new situations or petrified to leave the house?

You have the power to turn your dog into a good canine citizen and an ideal pet. But you have to start early on with the proper training and socialization. Between 6 and 12 weeks of age, puppies go through a developmental stage in which they need to be exposed to many new people or they may never become comfortable around unfamiliar humans. You'll also want to introduce your Miniature Schnauzer to other dogs, small animals, and maybe even larger animals like horses and cows. The more encounters your puppy has at a young age, the better his behavior will be when faced with new or unfamiliar situations.

During this stage of development, puppies also go through a "fear-imprint period." If they have a painful or traumatic experience with

SCHNAUZER SOCIALIZATION

Here are some ideas for socializing your Miniature Schnauzer:

- Take your dog for plenty of walks, and be sure to stop and say hi to neighbors.
- Take your dog to the pet store with you.

- Invite neighbor children to come play with your dog, under your supervision.
- Set up play dates with friendly neighbor dogs.
- Visit your veterinarian's office even when you don't have an appointment.
- Enroll in obedience training classes.

FAST FACT

Adequate socialization is very important for Miniature Schnauzer puppies. If you don't have children of your own, invite relatives' children or neighbors' children over for supervised play dates with your Miniature Schnauzer.

a certain stimulus, they are likely to develop a deep-rooted, generalized fear. For example, a puppy that has been hurt by a child during the fear-imprint period can easily become terrified of all children throughout his life.

Because of their herding and guarding background, Miniature Schnauzers are especially prone to becoming overly wary of strangers if they aren't properly socialized. Take your puppy out to see as many people, places, and other animals as possible, so he can learn to feel comfortable with them. In this way, your dog will learn how to use good judgment in his duties as a watchdog, instead of viewing everyone and everything outside the family as a potential threat.

Your Miniature Schnauzer may also go through a testy period during the "teenage" phase of his development, which occurs between six months and two years of age. At this stage, your dog may not listen very well. He may test his limits or appear obstinate. During this critical period, you should maintain a firm hand. If you consistently make it clear that you are the one in control, your dog will eventually develop a lifetime habit of obedience.

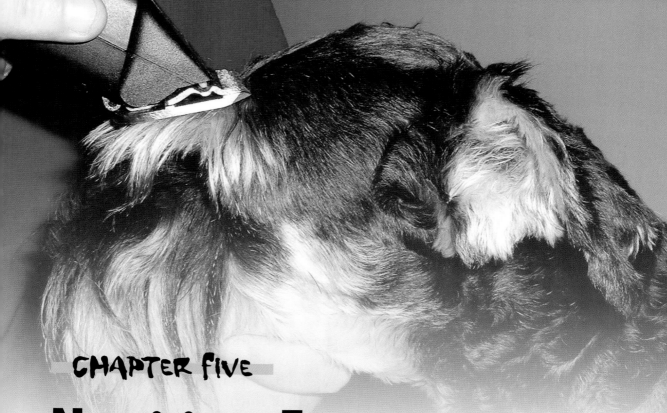

CHAPTER FIVE

Nutrition, Exercise, Grooming, and Training

Even though you've become smitten by the Miniature Schnauzer's dreamy charms, don't lose your foothold on the ground. Dogs are high-maintenance pets, and when you choose to own one, you've taken on a lot of responsibility.

The most labor-intensive activities are feeding, exercising, grooming, and training. Although these activities require time and energy, they offer many benefits as well. Studies have shown that people who own pets live longer and recuperate from illnesses more quickly than people who don't. Pets help give people purposeful lives, they are a good source of exercise, and, of course,

To look his best, a Miniature Schnauzer's coat will need to be clipped on a regular basis.

they provide an abundance of healing love. So just remember that fulfilling your Miniature Schnauzer's care requirements is as good for you as it is for your dog.

NURSING AND WEANING

Young puppies need the nutritional and immunological benefits provided by their mother's milk. This milk is high in nutrients, fat, and antibodies, which provide the kind of high-octane sustenance necessary for rapid growth and good health. Puppies are usually introduced to wet (canned) foods at four to five weeks of age, and they are introduced to solid (dry) foods at around six weeks of age. Even so, the weaning process is a gradual one, and puppies can still benefit from the dietary boost provided by their mother's milk up until they reach 8 to 10 weeks old.

By the age of eight weeks, a puppy is consuming sufficient amounts of solid foods to be weaned. This is a good time to bring your new puppy home. But once the canine apron strings are cut, what kind of food does a baby dog need?

COMMERCIALLY PREPARED DIETS

Like human babies, puppies have different nutritional needs from their adult counterparts. Even when weaned, puppies still need higher levels of nutrients and fat to promote healthy growth. That's why there are commercial dog foods formulated especially for puppies. In addition, most puppy foods are produced in a

A Miniature Schnauzer will eat as much as you allow, so don't just dump food into his bowl. Instead, measure carefully to make sure he is eating the proper amount. Otherwise, your dog is likely to become overweight or obese, which can lead to health problems.

smaller-size kibble, which is easier for small mouths to chew.

Your puppy will be ready for an adult-formula food between 10 and 12 months of age. When choosing either a puppy food or an adult food, you need to be a savvy shopper. There are dozens of commercially prepared dog foods on the market. When it comes to kibble, don't be impressed by fancy colors and cute shapes. These features are designed to appeal to people, not to dogs. Likewise, don't be swayed by attractive packaging or punchy advertising campaigns. The only way to really determine the quality of a commercial dog food is to read the ingredients label.

The first item on this list should be a meat product like chicken or beef. Quality foods use few if any grain products, and they often use natural forms of preservatives, like vitamins E and C. They also provide omega-3 and omega-6 fatty acids—usually in the form of fish oil or flaxseed oil—for good skin and coat condition.

Besides dry kibble, which should be the mainstay of your dog's diet, commercially prepared foods also come in canned and moist forms. Canned foods can contain up to 90 percent moisture, which means it would take an awful lot of it to meet

Although you should not leave food out for your Miniature Schnauzer to nibble throughout the day, you should make sure that he has plenty of water. To keep messes to a minimum, use a bowl that he won't be able to tip over when you're not around.

your dog's dietary requirements. However, Miniature Schnauzers especially appreciate the taste and softer texture, so feel free to supplement your dog's kibble with a couple spoonfuls.

Moist foods, which are often packaged in cellophane or pouches, usually contain undesirable additives to enhance flavor and prevent hardening. These might be fine for an occasional treat, but you should limit your dog's consumption of moist dog foods.

ALTERNATIVE DIETS

Commercially prepared diets for dogs have come a long way in the last couple decades. Quality has improved, and choices have multiplied. Still, there is a growing interest in alternative diets.

Some dog owners and experts recommend raw foods as the natural foundation for the canine diet. The popular Bones And Raw Food (BARF) diet is now available in the form of commercially packaged frozen patties. You simply thaw them out before feeding them to your dog. Although some owners prefer to prepare their own raw food meals for their dogs, the advantage of purchasing commercially packaged raw food is that all the necessary vitamins and supplements have already been added. Your dog's diet will be healthy and balanced.

Home-cooked diets have also gained many fans among dog lovers.

HEALTHY FEEDING PRACTICES

Choosing a good-quality food is only one part of ensuring that your Miniature Schnauzer gets proper nutrition. Take the following steps to establish healthy feeding practices:

- Measure your dog's food and adjust the amount as necessary to maintain your dog in good weight.
- Keep food and water dishes clean.
- Provide fresh water at all times.

- Feed your dog twice a day, at the same times every day.
- Do not leave food out for your dog to nibble on during the day. Remove any uneaten food after your dog has had 20 to 25 minutes to eat.
- Do not get in the habit of enhancing your dog's meals with human food.
- Limit your dog's consumption of treats, even during training.

FAST FACT

Good-quality pet foods often use vitamin E as a preservative. It may be listed as "mixed tocopherols" on the list of ingredients.

Basically, home-cooked dog food consists of "people food" such as meat, eggs, cottage cheese, and vegetables. Ingredients must be assembled in the right proportions, and vitamins and supplements must be added in order for the diet to be nutritionally complete.

Alternative diets may offer the opportunity to provide the healthiest food possible for your dog. But if you don't prepare the food properly, your dog may have a nutritionally inadequate diet. Do plenty of research on alternative diets before putting your Miniature Schnauzer on one.

EXERCISE

Perhaps the most time-consuming part of dog ownership involves giving your dog enough exercise. A dog that lies on the couch all day will suffer from poor fitness and be at risk

for weight gain. Dogs that don't get any exercise tend to develop behavior problems as well.

Miniature Schnauzers are athletic creatures. As such, they enjoy a good 20-minute aerobic workout in addition to a daily walk. A game of fetch, playtime with another dog, or any other activity that gets your dog running is a great way to give his cardiovascular system a workout and let him burn off excess energy. Exercise is particularly important for Miniature Schnauzers because they have a propensity to get a little chubby. Fortunately, your dog is small enough

Daily walks will keep your Miniature Schnauzer healthy and happy.

to do many such activities indoors as well as outdoors.

Exercise does not have to be a boring routine. Sometimes it's just a matter of including your dog in the same activities you enjoy. Take your dog with you when you jog, ride a bicycle, or hike. You'll both have fun and stay fit. And remember that the time you spend with your pet always contributes to a closer bond and a more fulfilling relationship.

GROOMING

Exercise helps keep your dog in good shape on the inside, but it's just as important to keep your dog in good shape on the outside. An unkempt Miniature Schnauzer can develop mats, skin problems, flea infestations, and all kinds of other problems. Nail care is necessary to prevent problems with your dog's feet and legs. Dental care is also required to maintain healthy teeth.

COAT CARE: The Miniature Schnauzer sports one of the canine world's most upscale coifs, which means a considerable amount of time and expense is involved in grooming. However, when properly maintained, a Schnauzer's coat is clean and attractive and will not shed.

Pet Schnauzers are trimmed quite short on the head and body, with longer hair left on the snout, eyebrows, legs, and underside. While most pet owners pay a professional dog groomer to do this trimming, you could do it yourself with the right equipment and a thorough study of the clipping pattern.

This diagram shows how a Miniature Schnauzer's body should be clipped. Using an electric razor with a detachable #10 clipper blade, start where the back of the skull meets the top of the neck, and clip all the way back to the tail. The neck and chest are clipped downward to a point approximately level with your dog's elbows (A). You can leave a slightly longer fringe between the legs, clipping from top to bottom. Clip the hair at the back of the rear legs downward, from the loin (B) to the stifle (C), then curving rearward above the hock (D).

If you decide to clip your own dog, there are several pieces of good advice to follow. First, buy a high-quality clipper and clipper blades. Cheaper models may make your dog uncomfortable with excessive noise, vibration, and snagging of the hair. Second, always use a blunt-tipped scissors in sensitive areas, like the groin or under the tail, until you have gained enough experience and confidence to use a clipper in these areas. And third, always brush and bathe your dog before clipping, as this will facilitate an easier, smoother clipping.

Miniature Schnauzers require clipping about every two to three months. With or without professional grooming, you'll still need to brush your dog weekly to keep his longer hair in manageable condition. A slicker brush or pin brush will be sufficient for this job. You may also need to clean your Miniature Schnauzer's beard daily, as food bits tend to accumulate there.

Because of the Miniature Schnauzer's short body clip, it's a good idea to provide a doggy coat for

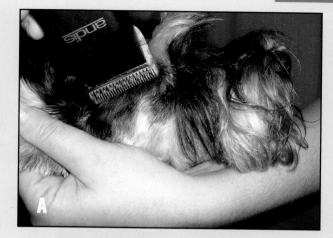

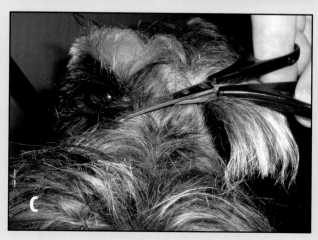

When trimming the head, start by clipping the hair above the eyebrows. Then, hold the dog's ears back (A) and clip downward between the ear and eyebrow. Use your hand to pull the beard hair forward (B) and clip the cheek. Next, clip the underside of the throat. Use a pair of short scissors (C) to trim the eyebrows and hair between the eyes.

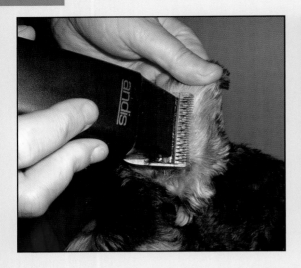 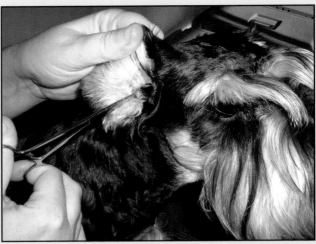

For an uncropped dog, use clippers to trim hair on the insides (left) and outsides of the ears. If necessary, you may need to use a hemostat (right) to pull hairs from your Miniature Schnauzer's ear canals.

your barbered buddy in wintertime. In very cold climates, this is a must, as smaller dogs do not have much body mass to generate warmth.

BATHING: Professional dog groomers usually include bathing as part of their grooming service. But if you decide to groom your own Miniature Schnauzer, or if your dog has gotten into some mess that requires a bath, the following tips will make bath time a little easier for you and your dog:

- Put a rubber mat in the sink or tub to prevent your dog from slipping and injuring himself.
- Assemble all your supplies ahead of time, so you don't have to search for them *after* your dog is wet.
- Keep one hand on your dog at all times.
- Do your best to keep soapsuds out of your dog's eyes.
- Prevent ear infections by keeping the inside of the ears dry with cotton balls.
- Be sure to rinse the coat thoroughly, as soap residue can cause a dull coat and itchy skin.

There are oodles of dog shampoos on the market, from color-enhancing shampoos to medicated shampoos. Unless you have a good reason to use a specialty shampoo, your best bet is to purchase the mildest shampoo you can find. It should provide a pleasant scent that appeals to you, because good-smelling dogs get lots of attention, and dogs that get lots of attention are happy dogs!

Some Miniature Schnauzers can be allowed to air dry after a vigorous towel rub. If your dog has particularly thick furnishings (feathered hair on the leg), you may want to expedite the process with a hair dryer on low setting.

NAIL CARE: Your Miniature Schnauzer's nails need to be trimmed about every three weeks. Failure to do so can result in foot, leg, and back problems for your dog, not to mention the scratches his long nails might accidentally inflict on you or on other people. If you are not comfortable clipping your dog's nails, veterinarians and professional groomers will do it for a reasonable fee.

To trim your dog's nails at home, you will need a pair of nail clippers that are specially made for dogs. There are also nail care products that allow you to grind off the nail gradually, so that you avoid removing too much.

The important thing to remember when clipping a dog's nails is to avoid cutting into the quick, which provides the blood supply to the nail. Doing so can cause pain and bleeding, so it's always preferable to cut a little bit of the nail at a time. Keep a blood clotting agent, such as a styptic pencil or styptic powder, on hand as you're clipping your pet's nails, and apply the coagulant immediately if you do cut the quick.

Whether you use a grinder or a more traditional scissors-type or guillotine-type clipper, a cooperative dog will make the chore of nail trimming

If you're not sure where the quick is when trimming your Miniature Schnauzer's nails, err on the side of caution. It is better to leave your dog's nails a little long than to cut the blood vessel, as this will cause pain and bleeding.

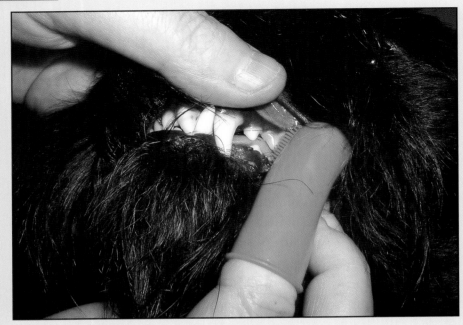

Use a finger brush and dog toothpaste to keep your Miniature Schnauzer's teeth clean. These supplies can be purchased at most pet stores. Don't try to save money by using your own toothpaste—your dog will dislike the minty flavor. Brush by gently massaging your dog's teeth and gums for a few minutes each day.

much easier. Touch and hold your Miniature Schnauzer's feet while you're petting, playing, and grooming him. This will get him used to having his feet handled. If your dog shows an aversion to the nail clipper, perform frequent "mock" nail clippings by pretending to clip his nails until he becomes desensitized to the process. Treats for good behavior will give your dog even more incentive to tolerate nail clipping.

DENTAL CARE: Small dogs are much more prone to dental problems, and the Miniature Schnauzer is no exception. Your dog will require regular teeth brushing, and your veterinarian should perform periodic dental checkups.

A variety of products are available for cleaning canine teeth. They include toothbrushes, finger applicators, liver-flavored toothpaste, and dental wipes. The real trick is to convince your dog that it's in his best interest to cooperate.

Introduce teeth brushing in a slow, positive way, by brushing just a few teeth at a time. Lavish your dog with praise for good behavior, and give him a very special treat afterward. A bone or dental toy filled with stuffing will give your pet something to look forward to and give his teeth brushing a good finishing touch.

Your veterinarian may recommend a professional teeth cleaning from time to time. This thorough cleaning will remove accumulated tartar and plaque, which can cause potentially dangerous infections, severe pain, and loss of teeth.

HOUSETRAINING

Your dog is constantly learning. If he doesn't learn the right things, he may never become a very good pet. That's why good training is so important.

One of the first and most crucial things your puppy needs to learn is housetraining. Even formerly house-trained adult dogs may experience a lapse in housetraining when they are adopted into a new home. Although housetraining can sometimes be frustrating, there are ways to make it easier for both you and your dog.

First, you need to have reasonable expectations. Puppies don't have much bladder control until they are several months old. Be patient, and don't put an arbitrary limit on how long housetraining should take.

Second, to housetrain your Miniature Schnauzer with a minimum of accidents, remember that

Put your Miniature Schnauzer on a regular eating schedule, and give him frequent opportunities to use the designated outdoor potty area.

FAST FACT

Puppies need to use the potty frequently. As a rule of thumb, a puppy can hold it one hour for every month of his age. A two-month-old puppy can hold it for up to two hours, a three-month-old puppy for three hours, and so on. Always keep in mind, however, that eating, sleeping, and exercising also influence your puppy's need to eliminate.

prevention is the key. Always observe your dog carefully when he is allowed to explore freely in your house, and keep him confined when you can't supervise him. Your dog can't get into the habit of messing in your house if you never give him the opportunity to do it.

Third, help your dog succeed by establishing a designated outdoor potty area. Take your dog to the same spot every day so he learns to associate that area with its intended purpose. Be sure to take him there when he is most likely to go, such as after napping, eating, or playing. Treats for eliminating in the proper area can further encourage your dog to meet your housetraining goals.

If you catch your dog in the act of eliminating in the house, scoop him up quickly and rush him to his outdoor spot. Don't punish him for accidents, as doing so will likely make him fearful and less capable of learning. Treat your dog kindly during the housetraining process, ignore mistakes, and clean up messes without a fuss. With plenty of positive reinforcement, your dog will become housetrained.

CRATE TRAINING

Crate training has many benefits to offer. A crate-trained dog can be confined in his crate for short periods when his owner can't be there to supervise him. He can be transported safely in a crate to dog shows, veterinary clinics, or vacation destinations. The crate can also provide a private, protected place for your dog to eat or sleep, away from the harassment of children or other pets.

Although dogs are instinctually programmed to prefer den-like places to sleep, as their ancestors lived in dens, this preference isn't automatically transferred to crates. Because of this, dogs that are not

FAST FACT

Puppies will quickly become confused if you allow a behavior one day but not the next. Make sure you are consistent with your new friend.

crate trained may put up an enormous fuss when they are confined to a crate.

You'll need to proceed slowly when crate training your Miniature Schnauzer. Expecting more from your dog than he is able to give will ultimately make him fearful of the crate, and it will sabotage your training efforts. In the beginning, spend a little time every day helping your dog to feel comfortable with the crate. Put toys or treats near the door of the crate, and encourage your pup to fetch them. As your dog gains com-

fort and confidence, you can start putting toys or treats inside the crate until your dog is willing to enter it on his own.

When you are not training, leave the crate open for your dog to explore. Make it as comfortable and as enticing as possible with a soft pad and toys. Your dog may just decide by himself that the crate is a desirable, special place.

When you think your dog is ready, you can start closing the crate's door for short periods. Make this phase of training as easy as possible for your

Treats provide a good incentive when training a dog. However, limit the number of treats that you feed to your Miniature Schnauzer, as overfeeding can cause obesity.

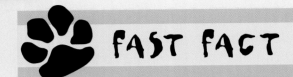

FAST FACT

Enrollment in an obedience class has many advantages, including the support and guidance of a professional trainer; the opportunity to train your dog in a distracting environment, which can make your dog more reliable; and the chance for you and your dog to socialize with other dogs and dog lovers.

pet by providing a treat-releasing toy or some other distraction to keep him busy for a while. And when you are ready to release him from his crate, always wait until he is quiet before opening the door. If you release your dog when he is fussing, he'll learn to fuss in order to get out—the exact behavior you're trying to discourage. Eventually, you should be able to leave your dog in his crate for longer periods.

GOOD MANNERS

Almost any dog can make a good companion, but a trained dog makes a great companion. Dogs that have good manners are a joy, not only for their owners but also for other people who meet them. So teach your dog the following rules of behavior, and begin this training as soon as you bring your dog home.

"Out" is a very handy command to instruct your dog to get out of restricted areas. This can be used indoors or outdoors, and it can help

CHOOSING A TRAINING CENTER

When evaluating a training center, always visit the center in person and obtain answers to the following questions:

- Does the trainer use positive training methods? (Punishment should never be used in the process of training.)
- Is the trainer as good with people as he or she is with dogs?
- Does the trainer appear to be knowledgeable about canine behavior?
- Do the class participants appear to be enjoying their experience?
- Do the dogs appear to be motivated to learn?
- Does the class consist of no more than eight dogs?
- Are the training sessions limited to an hour?

in yard boundary training. Usher your dog out of forbidden areas while saying "out." Rewards should be offered only when your dog respects his boundaries. You can test your dog on this skill by carrying one of his toys into a forbidden area and seeing whether he follows you. Usher your dog out of the area if he follows you; reward him if he does not.

Use the "wait" command to prevent a zealous dog from rushing out doorways or jumping into his food dish before it has been placed on the floor. Practice this command with your Miniature Schnauzer on a leash. Say "wait," and allow him to go through the door or eat his food only after you issue a release word, such as "OK." The "wait" command can be used anytime your dog goes through a door, including at the vet's office or when disembarking from your vehicle.

"Off" should be used whenever you need your dog to vacate a piece of furniture. Dogs with manners learn that couches are for people first and dogs second. Insist that your dog remove himself from furniture when you instruct him to do so. Take him by the collar and gently remove him if he fails to comply. Be sure to provide a soft dog bed on the floor so your dog has a comfortable place of his own in which to recline.

Making your Miniature Schnauzer sit in order to get a treat will make it easier to teach him other skills.

BASIC OBEDIENCE

Your Miniature Schnauzer must learn a number of basic obedience commands in order to meet the minimum requirements of a trained dog. These commands are also the foundation of any type of advanced training you might want to pursue. Be prepared to spend at least 15 minutes three times

Dogs must be trained not to tug or pull incessantly against their leash. You'll also want your Miniature Schnauzer to walk at your left side, and to stop walking when you do.

per week training your dog to master these skills.

"Come" is by far the most important command to teach your dog. This skill takes time and practice beyond your normal training sessions. It should be practiced constantly. Call your dog to you by saying "come," and reward him with a treat each time he does come. If you issue the "come" command but don't get a prompt response, refrain from issuing the command again. Doing so will only teach your dog that he can ignore this vital command. If your dog does not come, he simply does not get rewarded. You can practice this skill indoors as well as outdoors, with your dog in a fenced area or on a long leash to keep him safe. And you can encourage your dog to comply by clapping your hands, running in the opposite direction—dogs love to chase—and using a happy, excited voice. Don't make the mistake of punishing your dog if he does not come. This will discourage him from coming the next time you call him.

"Sit" is a very easy command to teach most dogs. Hold a treat just above your dog's head so he looks up to see it. Then move the treat toward your dog's rear just a bit. As his eyes follow the path of the treat, your dog may automatically drop into a sitting position. When this happens, give him the treat immediately. Soon he'll learn what you want him to do when you say "sit."

"Down" is a little more challenging for some dogs, but you can lure your Miniature Schnauzer into this position by first getting him to sit. Then hold a treat on the floor in front of him. Draw the treat away from him until your dog stretches out into a "down" position. Do this training gradually, and reward your dog for even a small amount of progress until he lies down on command.

"Stay" is another skill that needs to be learned gradually. Put your dog in a "sit" or "down" position, then say "stay." Wait only a moment, and if he doesn't move, reward him immediately with a treat. Gradually increase the amount of time you require your Miniature Schnauzer to refrain from moving, and increase your distance from him when you issue the "stay" command. If your dog keeps moving before you give him the OK, it means the training is progressing too fast. Shorten the time and distance, and make sure

your dog has thoroughly mastered the command with the easier parameters before increasing the time or distance again.

"Heel," which requires your dog to walk precisely at your left side, and the less formal "walk nice," which requires your dog to walk on a loose leash, are invaluable commands. It's no fun to walk a dog that pulls constantly on the leash. To teach your dog the "walk nice" command, say the command and stop dead in your tracks when your dog pulls on his leash. Refuse to proceed until your Miniature Schnauzer releases tension on the leash. Your dog will eventually turn around to look at you and put slack in the leash so you can continue. If you respond consistently whenever your dog pulls, he will soon learn that pulling won't get him anywhere—literally.

For the more disciplined "heel," turn around and walk in the opposite direction whenever your dog pulls. As he comes to your side to catch up with you, say "heel" and reward him. You can further encourage your Miniature Schnauzer to master this skill by holding a treat at your left side and rewarding him occasionally for maintaining his position there.

CHAPTER SIX

Health Issues Your Dog May Face

Regardless of the jobs they were bred to do, many Miniature Schnauzers think they have a duty to spread their joie de vivre throughout the world. Fulfilling this desire requires a lot of energy and passion, but it also requires something else—good health.

CHOOSING A VETERINARIAN

Keeping your Miniature Schnauzer healthy is a big responsibility that

---

If you're a novice dog owner, recommendations from friends or family members can help you find the right vet for your pet.

cannot be accomplished alone. You'll need to form a partnership with a veterinarian. But how do you choose the right veterinarian?

Every veterinarian has the academic qualifications to provide adequate health care for your pet, but each veterinarian has his or her own strengths and weaknesses. The quest is not to find a perfect veterinarian, but to find the perfect veterinarian for *you*. This is why, even when considering a veterinarian who has been referred to you by a friend, family member, coworker, or breeder, you still need to evaluate the veterinarian on your own terms.

Some things you want to keep in mind while investigating veterinarians in your area are: Does the veterinarian treat you and your dog with kindness and respect? Does the veterinarian explain things to you in terms you can understand? Does the veterinarian take the time to answer your questions and address your concerns? Does the veterinarian have experience with the Miniature Schnauzer breed?

In addition, veterinary hospitals vary considerably. Do the hospital's operating hours include any weeknights or weekends? If not, is there an emergency clinic nearby to handle emergencies? Does the hospital have any specialized diagnostic equipment,

Ideally, a prospective veterinary clinic should be a member of the American Animal Hospital Association or a similar organization that inspects and accredits veterinary facilities.

such as ultrasound or heart monitoring equipment? And what do they charge for routine veterinary care, like office charges, exams, vaccinations, and spaying or neutering surgery?

After considering all these factors, you'll be able to make an informed decision about your dog's veterinary care. This will give you considerable peace of mind.

THE FIRST VETERINARY EXAM

Regardless of where you obtained your Miniature Schnauzer, or whether

Look for a veterinary clinic that is located close to your home. If your Miniature Schnauzer has a medical emergency, you'll want to get to the clinic within 20 to 30 minutes.

you purchased a puppy or adopted an adult dog, you should schedule your dog's first veterinary appointment immediately after bringing your new companion home. You'll want to determine your dog's health status as soon as possible, before your heart-strings have grown too strong or health guarantees have expired.

There are a number of things you should be prepared to bring to this first exam. In order to check for internal parasites, your veterinarian will need a small stool sample from your dog. Make a list of any questions you have concerning your dog's health and behavior and take it with you. And lastly, bring all medical records you have for your dog, including vaccination records, rabies certificates, exam dates, test results, or any previous medical treatments or surgeries. This information will be invaluable to your vet in evaluating your dog's health.

The first veterinary exam is also a good time to obtain necessary vacci-nations, worming treatments, or heartworm preventive. These routine health care procedures will give your dog a good start toward a healthy lifestyle, the benefits of which can be profound.

VACCINATIONS

Vaccinations are particularly beneficial to your Miniature Schnauzer's health because they help prevent some very serious and potentially deadly diseases. The specific vaccinations your dog needs will depend on where you live and your dog's risk of exposure. Even so, there are several highly contagious and especially devastating diseases for which vaccination is recommended for all dogs. These core vaccines include rabies, distemper, parvovirus, and canine adenovirus-2. The rabies vaccine is always given as a separate inocula-tion, but the others are often combined into a single-dose injection.

CANINE ADENOVIRUS: There are two forms of canine adenovirus. Canine adenovirus-1 causes infectious canine hepatitis, which affects the dog's liver and kidneys. The most obvious symptom is jaundice, which causes a yellowish pigment of the skin or eyes. Other symptoms may include a swollen belly and vomiting. There is a vaccine for canine adenovirus-1, but it is not recommended because of the risk of serious adverse reactions. However, protection against canine adenovirus-1 is conferred by the vaccine for canine adenovirus-2, which is a mild respiratory disease. This vaccine is recommended for all dogs.

DISTEMPER: A highly contagious viral disease, distemper is most often fatal for puppies, though it can also kill adult dogs. The disease causes discharge of the eyes and nose, fever, vomiting, diarrhea, and severe lethargy. At some point in their lives, almost all dogs will be exposed to the virus that causes distemper, and there is no cure for the disease. This is why it's imperative that you vaccinate your Miniature Schnauzer.

KENNEL COUGH: Kennel cough is a highly contagious respiratory

FAST FACT

Vaccine protocols change periodically as more research is done on canine immunity. A majority of veterinarians now recommend three-year booster vaccinations rather than annual boosters for most vaccines. Check the American Animal Hospital Association Web site (www.aahavet.org) for the most recent vaccination guidelines.

condition characterized by a dry, hacking cough. It is caused primarily by the bacterium *Bordetella bronchiseptica*, often in combination with the parainfluenza and canine adenovirus-2 viruses. The intranasal bordetella vaccine protects against all three agents. Since kennel cough is commonly spread among dogs housed in groups, vaccination is recommended for any dog that comes in contact with other dogs—for example, in training classes or at dog shows.

LEPTOSPIROSIS: A bacterial infection that affects the liver and kidneys, leptospirosis produces symptoms of fever, jaundice, and excessive water consumption. The vaccine for leptospirosis is not considered a core vaccine, and vaccination may only be necessary in areas where outbreaks have occurred. Nevertheless, some veterinarians consider the symptoms worrisome enough to warrant vaccination as a precaution.

LYME DISEASE: Lyme disease is a bacterial infection transmitted by ticks. The symptoms can vary greatly from one individual to another but often include stiffness, lameness, swelling of the joints, swelling or redness at the site of the tick bite, and general malaise. The Lyme disease

vaccine is recommended for any dog that lives in or travels to areas where ticks are present.

PARAINFLUENZA: Like a human flu virus, canine parainfluenza causes respiratory symptoms such as coughing and nasal discharge. While parainfluenza is usually not deadly by itself, it is highly contagious and can lead to pneumonia or a weakened immune system, which is why many veterinarians recommend vaccination.

PARVOVIRUS: Parvovirus is another potentially fatal disease that is most dangerous for puppies. It affects the gastrointestinal system and can cause bloody diarrhea, high fevers, vomiting, and lethargy. Dogs that survive the disease can be left with permanent damage. The parvovirus vaccine can keep your dog safe.

RABIES: By law, all dogs in North America must have rabies vaccinations, though the protocols vary by municipality and state. Your veterinarian can tell you what the rabies requirements are for your area.

EXTERNAL PARASITES

Ticks are small brown parasites that tend to live in wooded or grassy areas. Ticks attach themselves to animals or people, implanting their heads under the skin to feed on blood. In the process, they can transmit diseases, such as Lyme disease.

If you live in an area where ticks are prevalent, you can minimize your dog's exposure by keeping your dog out of tall grass during tick season— usually from late spring through summer. Check your dog daily for ticks by giving him a thorough petting. Remove any ticks you find by grasping them close to their heads with tweezers and pulling them off quickly. Be sure to disinfect your hands, the tweezers, and the bite site.

There are a number of very effective topical products you can use to kill and repel ticks. These are usually applied to a spot of skin on your dog's back. An added benefit of these treatments is that they can also provide protection against fleas.

Fleas are annoying little parasites that also subsist on the blood of a host animal. They can cause a tremendous amount of discomfort. Intense itching can lead to skin damage from scratching. Fleas also transmit tapeworms to pets.

Always address any flea problem immediately, as a small infestation can quickly mushroom into a parasitic nightmare. Preventive treatments are highly recommended in

Check your dog carefully for ticks after he plays in high grass or wooded areas. These tiny parasites can spread dangerous diseases to your Miniature Schnauzer.

warmer climates where fleas proliferate easily. If your dog gets fleas, you'll have to treat all the pets in your household, as well as your home and yard, in order to get the problem under control. Many flea-eradication products are available, but if you have difficulties getting rid of an infestation, consult your veterinarian.

He or she will be able to recommend an effective plan of action.

Not all external parasites are visible to the naked eye, as are ticks and fleas. A number of mite species can proliferate unseen on your pet's skin. If you notice any patchy hair loss, itching, skin irritation, poor coat condition, or flaky skin, always take your dog to the veterinarian for a proper diagnosis. Damage caused by external parasites is easier to remedy when your dog gets prompt treatment.

THE DANGER OF HEARTWORMS

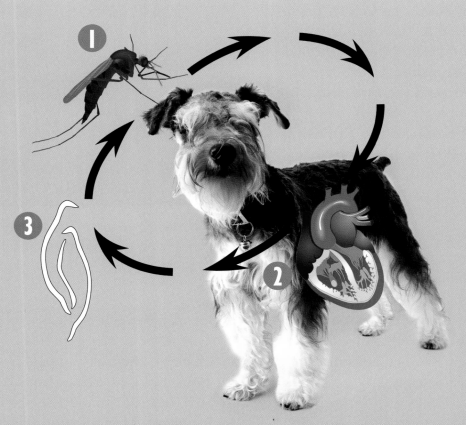

Heartworms are a concern for all dog owners. The graphic above illustrates the cycle of heartworm development. When a mosquito (1) bites a Miniature Schnauzer, it can inject microfilaria into his bloodstream. The microfilaria travel through the bloodstream to the heart (2), where they grow into heartworms (3) and multiply, clogging the dog's heart. If left untreated, heartworms can kill.

INTERNAL PARASITES

Some parasites live inside the body, but their effects on your dog's health can still produce visible external symptoms. Intestinal worms can cause a pot-bellied appearance and dull coat, along with suppressed energy level, especially in puppies. Heartworms are indicated by coughing, difficulty breathing, loss of stamina, or collapse. In both cases, prevention is infinitely preferable to treatment after symptoms appear.

Intestinal parasites that can afflict your Miniature Schnauzer include roundworms (which are the most common), hookworms, whipworms, and tapeworms. All have complicated life cycles that eventually culminate in an adult stage inside the dog's intestine. Puppies can acquire intestinal worms from their mother's milk or, in some cases, before they are even born. It is essential that all puppies receive treatment for intestinal worms. Adult dogs can pick up intestinal worms in a number of ways—from the soil, from an infected animal's feces, or from ingesting the carcass of a wild animal. In the case of tapeworms, they are transmitted to dogs by fleas.

An annual fecal exam by your veterinarian can help detect the presence of intestinal worms and determine the appropriate treatment. Be aware that not all worming treatments are effective against all worms. Tapeworms, in particular, require specialized treatment.

Heartworms are another worm-type parasite. This deadly invader, which is spread by mosquitoes, targets the cardiopulmonary systems of dogs. The adult worms can grow to 6 inches (15 cm) in length within a dog's heart and populate to the point of causing serious cardiac distress and eventually death. Any dog that lives in areas where mosquitoes reside should receive regular heartworm preventives.

COMMON HEALTH PROBLEMS

The Miniature Schnauzer is tenacious in both spirit and body. Although robust, the breed is not exempt from common canine health problems. Since many health conditions have a hereditary link, it's very important to choose a Miniature Schnauzer with care. But if you are

FAST FACT

Roundworms are often passed on to people, especially children. Have your dog checked regularly for intestinal worms.

not certain of the quality of your Miniature Schnauzer's breeding, you should at least become familiar with various common health conditions so that you can recognize their symptoms and seek prompt veterinary care for your pet.

EYE DISORDERS: Several hereditary problems can affect your pet's vision. Cataracts, distichiasis, entropion, and progressive retinal atrophy have all been known to occur in the Miniature Schnauzer breed.

Cataracts are opaque obstructions that form in the eye lens. Some cataracts remain relatively small and create minimal barriers to vision. Others can result in blindness. Surgery is the only effective treatment for cataracts. In severe cases the diseased lens can be replaced with an artificial one, but this procedure requires the expertise of a veterinary ophthalmologist and is quite expensive.

Distichiasis is a hereditary condition that involves the growth of abnormal hairs on the eyelid. When these hairs grow into and rub against the eye, they can cause injury and vision-reducing scarring. Mild cases may not require treatment, but if eye injury occurs, surgery is required to correct the condition.

Entropion is another hereditary condition that affects the eyelid. Dogs with this condition have eyelids that roll inward, causing the eyelashes to abrade the cornea. As with dis-

When a Miniature Schnauzer has hereditary congenital cataracts, they occur in both eyes. The cataracts can be seen at birth, although they do not become fully opaque until a Miniature Schnauzer is one to three years old.

tichiasis, injury and scarring to the cornea can result in vision impairment. Young dogs with this condition may have their eyelids "tacked" into the correct position so they will grow normally. Older dogs may require surgery to correct the problem.

The most devastating eye condition that affects Miniature Schnauzers is progressive retinal atrophy (PRA). No medical treatment or surgery can prevent the ultimate outcome of this condition: total blindness. The dire prognosis makes it imperative that you ask your Miniature Schnauzer's breeder about genetic testing for PRA.

SKIN DISORDERS: If your Miniature Schnauzer seems itchy in the absence of external parasites, he may have an allergy. Along with the scratching, your dog may suffer symptoms of patchy hair loss, rashes, or skin lesions. The allergen causing your dog's skin problems may be a chemical, a food product, or inhaled particles such as pollen. Your veterinarian can perform allergy tests or direct you to change your dog's environment or diet in order to identify the culprit. Almost all cases of canine allergies can be managed with help from a vet.

While allergies tend to affect many different dog breeds, one skin condition is linked primarily to Schnauzers: Schnauzer comedo syndrome. This condition causes acne-like blackheads to form along the dog's back. Serious cases may result in itching, hair loss, and bacterial infections of the skin. Although not curable, Schnauzer comedo syndrome can be managed with the use of acne products, anti-seborrheic shampoos, and medications.

ENDOCRINE DISORDERS: Loss of hair isn't always an indication of a skin disorder; imbalances in the endocrine system can also result in itchiness and bald spots. The most common endocrine disorder in dogs is lymphocytic thyroiditis, an autoimmune disease that causes the body to attack its own thyroid gland. As the gland is destroyed, the thyroid can no longer produce adequate levels of hormones, a condition called hypothyroidism.

Besides patchy hair loss, this condition can cause a variety of symptoms. Some dogs may gain weight, have difficulty tolerating cold temperatures, or suffer a lack of energy. A daily supplement of hormones allows affected dogs to live long and productive lives.

Cushing's disease, also known as hyperadrenocorticism, is another endocrine disorder that can cause a wide range of symptoms in the Miniature Schnauzer. Some of the most common symptoms are hair loss, increased appetite, increased water consumption, and abdominal enlargement resulting in a potbellied appearance.

Most cases of Cushing's disease are caused by a tumor of the pituitary gland, which in turn causes the pituitary to produce too much glucocorticoid in the body. This condition is most often managed with oral medications. The medications are costly, and once started they must be administered for the remainder of the dog's life.

BLEEDING DISORDERS: Two bleeding disorders occasionally affect Miniature Schnauzers: hemophilia A (also known as factor VIII deficiency) and von Willebrand disease. Both conditions prevent blood from clotting normally and can lead to profuse bleeding or bruising. Like hemophilia in humans, hemophilia A in dogs is a sex-linked trait that is carried by females but affects mostly males. Von Willebrand disease affects both genders equally.

Treatment for bleeding disorders depends on the severity of the condition. Miniature Schnauzers with mild forms of these diseases can often live normal lives without treatment. If the dog sustains a serious injury or requires surgery, however, a blood transfusion may be necessary. Dogs with more serious forms of hemophilia A or von Willebrand disease may need frequent transfusions. There is no cure for either condition, so steps should be taken to minimize the chance of injury to affected dogs.

ORTHOPEDIC DISORDERS: The Miniature Schnauzer, like many other small dog breeds, is affected by Legg-Calve-Perthes disease. This orthopedic disorder is caused by an inadequate blood supply to the head of the femur, or thighbone, at the hip joint. Eventually, the bone begins to die off, the cartilage becomes deformed, and the hip joint becomes beset with arthritis and inflammation. The pain caused by this condition is manifested by symptoms of limping, skipping with the hind legs, or chewing at the affected area.

When the femoral head retains enough of its natural shape to function properly, Legg-Calve-Perthes disease may be managed with exercise restrictions and medications for pain and inflammation. In other cases, surgery is the only way to relieve pain and restore a functioning joint.

OTHER DISORDERS: Kidney and liver problems are common in the

Reputable breeders have their Miniature Schnauzers tested for hereditary disorders, and do not breed dogs with the potential to produce offspring with genetic problems.

Miniature Schnauzer. If your dog shows symptoms of jaundice, abdominal swelling, or discolored urine or feces, he may be suffering from liver disease. Kidney problems will be indicated by excessive water consumption, excessive urination, and weight loss. These are all signs that your little buddy needs to see a veterinarian.

Also, watch for an acute onset of bloody diarrhea, as the Miniature Schnauzer is particularly prone to hemorrhagic gastroenteritis, a digestive condition that can result in life-threatening shock. Veterinary treatment and a change in diet can minimize the severity of this condition and help prevent its recurrence.

The Miniature Schnauzer is also afflicted with bladder stones more frequently than other breeds. Symptoms include straining to urinate, pain or whimpering during urination, or blood in the urine. If you

This salt and pepper Miniature Schnauzer has cropped ears and a docked tail. The practice of ear cropping originated to protect the dog from injury, because long, floppy ears could easily be grabbed and damaged by the rodents a Miniature Schnauzer was bred to hunt and kill. Tails were shortened, or docked, for a similar reason—damage to the tail does not heal easily and can eventually affect a dog's overall health. However, ear cropping and tail docking are painful for the dog, and since today few Miniature Schnauzers are used for their original purpose, some dog owners opt not to have the procedure performed on their dogs.

observe any of these, seek prompt veterinary attention for your pooch.

CROPPING AND DOCKING

Most veterinary care is designed to keep a dog healthy. However, Miniature Schnauzers often undergo cosmetic surgery—specifically, ear cropping and tail docking. Since docking is generally performed when a puppy is only a few days old, this procedure is usually done at the breeder's discretion.

Cropping, on the other hand, can be performed at just about any age, though the chances of a successful and attractive outcome are greatest when done before a puppy reaches 12 weeks of age. Some breeders will have their Miniature Schnauzer puppies cropped as early as 8 weeks of age.

If your puppy was not cropped when you got him, you'll need to make the decision as to whether or not you will have this done. This is not a decision you should take lightly. The procedure does cause pain for

CROPPING TIPS

- Choose a veterinarian who specializes in this procedure.
- Ask breeders or breed club members for veterinarian referrals.
- Ask the veterinarian for references.
- Be aware of the postoperative care involved.

the dog. As with any type of surgery, there are medical risks, and cropping requires lengthy postoperative care— at least three weeks of ear wrapping.

If you decide to have your Miniature Schnauzer cropped, make sure you discuss the risks thoroughly with your veterinarian. If your dog is not intended to be a show dog, there is nothing wrong with opting for the "softer" look of an uncropped Schnauzer. Miniature Schnauzers possess an irrepressible cuteness, regardless of the type of ears they wear!

CHAPTER SEVEN

Enjoying Your Miniature Schnauzer

Your Miniature Schnauzer was bred to be a superb companion. But your dog can do so much more than simply keep you company. Consider sharing activities with your little buddy. Both of your lives will be enriched immensely.

Training is one of the most rewarding activities you can do with your Miniature Schnauzer. Training builds trust. It increases communication and strengthens the human-canine bond. Each time your highly intelligent Miniature Schnauzer masters a new skill, both of you will enjoy a sense of accomplishment. Best of all, just about any type of training will further the development of a more responsive, better-behaved pet.

Miniature Schnauzers will always appreciate the time you spend playing with them.

AKC CANINE GOOD CITIZEN: In its efforts to promote responsible dog ownership and the acceptance of dogs as good citizens, the AKC offers certification for any dog that passes the AKC Canine Good Citizen (CGC) test. This test is also the foundation of training for dogs approved for therapy work through Therapy Dogs International (TDI).

To earn a CGC certificate, dogs are tested on basic obedience and social skills. The dog owners are evaluated on the care and appearance of their dogs, as well as their appropriate handling of their dogs.

Many dog training facilities now offer training classes to work on CGC skills. You can enroll in a class or teach the skills to your dog on your own, but the test itself must be administered by an approved CGC evaluator. For a complete list of test skills, or to locate an evaluator in your area, see the AKC Web site (www.akc.org).

OBEDIENCE: Obedience is another wonderful training activity. If you enjoy competing, showing off your dog, and socializing with other dog owners, this may be the canine sport for you. Because of their compliant nature and their intelligence, Miniature Schnauzers are great candidates to excel at obedience trials.

The AKC sponsors obedience trials at various levels of difficulty, with opportunities to earn titles as your dog proceeds through each level. Even at the novice level, mastering the skill set can be challenging. Your dog will have to learn to heel on and off leash, obey the "stay" command while in a group of dogs, and stand for examination, in addition to other basic obedience commands. When your dog executes these skills adequately, he'll earn a Companion Dog (CD) title.

Titles earned in obedience are customarily listed in their abbreviated form after a dog's registered name. Other obedience titles include Companion Dog Excellent (CDX), which is offered at the open level; and Utility Dog (UD) and Utility Dog Excellent (UDX), which are earned at the utility level. If you are really ambitious, you can continue to compete at the utility level to gain points toward the coveted Obedience Trial Champion (OTCh) title.

CANINE SPORTS

Obedience is not the only organized activity that offers titles for dogs. Agility, flyball, canine musical freestyle, and Earthdog trials all provide opportunities for your dog to excel. If you have the energy and motivation, there is no reason you

Miniature Schnauzers possess the speed and strength needed to excel in agility competitions.

can't train your Miniature Schnauzer in more than one sport.

AGILITY: Your lively little dog has considerable aptitude for the high-energy sport of agility. Agility dogs must traverse a course that consists of tunnels, jumps, weave poles, and other obstacles. The goal is to complete the course in the fastest time with the fewest penalties for faults. Ribbons are awarded to the first-through fourth-place finishers.

If you are thinking about getting involved in competitive agility, bear in mind that the energy requirement for this sport doesn't just apply to your dog. The course layout for every event is different, and you'll have to run along the course to direct your Miniature Schnauzer to each obstacle. Agility can be a great way for you to stay active and fit.

Teaching your dog how to negotiate the agility obstacles also requires a substantial training commitment. The easiest way to learn how to train your dog for the sport is to enroll in an agility training class.

Even for dog owners who aren't interested in competition, agility can be a great way to provide exercise and mental stimulation to a canine companion. Many dog owners practice agility in their own backyards.

To learn more about this fun canine activity, visit the Web site of the United States Dog Agility Association (www.usdaa.com) or the North American Dog Agility Council (www.nadac.com).

FLYBALL: The training for flyball isn't quite as intensive as the training for agility. Still, flyball is an action-packed sport. It requires the dog to run a straight 51-foot (15.5 m) course that includes four jumps and a ball launcher at the end. When the dog gets to the ball launcher, he steps on a pedal that releases a ball. The dog has to retrieve the ball and bring it back through the course to his handler. Flyball is a team sport, with four dogs on each team running in a relay.

To learn how to get involved in the sport, contact a local flyball club. The North American Flyball Association provides a list of clubs at its Web site (www.flyball.org).

CANINE MUSICAL FREESTYLE: Canine musical freestyle and its sister sport, heelwork to music, are the newest and most interesting of canine sports. They combine music with various obedience maneuvers. The result is a wonderful display of the human-canine partnership. In the case of canine musical freestyle, the entertainment is enhanced with costumes and tricks.

If your Miniature Schnauzer is a born performer, you might want to consider canine musical freestyle. If you've never seen a freestyle performance, you can watch some routines on YouTube. While training classes for freestyle are still unavailable in many areas, there are a number of books and videos that you can consult. Check the Web site of the World Canine Freestyle Organization (www.worldcaninefreestyle.org) for more information or to find a freestyle club in your area.

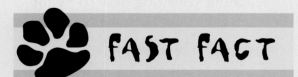

FAST FACT

Canine agility made its debut at the Crufts Dog Show in Britain in 1979. It has since grown to become one of the most popular dog sports in the world.

EARTHDOG TRIALS: The Miniature Schnauzer's well-developed prey drive is a tremendous asset in Earthdog trials. Even though the Schnauzer's ancestry is removed from that of typical terriers, many Schnauzers are willing to "go to ground" with terrier-like tenacity in the pursuit of vermin.

Earthdog trials are offered by the AKC and the American Working Terrier Association (AWTA). Underground tunnels are constructed with a number of turns, entrances, and dead ends, depending on the level of competition. Dogs are required to follow the scent of a rat through the tunnel to find the cage of rats at the end. This is an exciting sport for both dogs and their owners. If this sounds like something your

THE COSTS OF COMPETITION

If you decide to get involved in competition sports with your Miniature Schnauzer, the annual cost of caring for your dog will skyrocket, as you add on the following expenses:

Entry fees: $20 to $30 for each class entered. Depending on which sports and how many you compete in with your dog, entry fees for a show or trial can run from $20 to $100, or more.

Transportation: Fuel for your car or motor home to drive to shows within driving distance, and plane fare for important shows farther from home, such as the American Miniature Schnauzer Club's annual National Specialty show.

Lodging: Hotel or motel rooms range from $80 to several hundred dollars a night, depending on quality, location, and whether or not the pet fee charged by the hotel is refundable. At some events, participants are permitted to camp on the show grounds. If you own a motor home or camping trailer, this option usually costs from $15 to $50 a night.

Meals away from home: Budget appropriately, depending on your appetite and tastes.

Handler's fees: $100 to $600 or more per show. Hiring a professional handler to exhibit your Miniature Schnauzer in conformation events, instead of handling him yourself, can increase your dog's success in the show ring, but the cost of earning those awards will increase as well.

Photographs of wins: When your dog wins at a show, captures a title, or earns a perfect score, you will want to get a photograph to remember the day. Sponsoring clubs arrange to have one or more professional photographers on site at the show to provide that service to exhibitors. Dog show photographers generally charge between $25 and $35 per print.

Miniature Schnauzer was born to do, consult the AKC Web site (www.akc.org) or the AWTA Web site (www.dirt-dog.com) to find out how you can participate.

SHOWING AND BREEDING

Perhaps you've become so enamored of the Miniature Schnauzer breed that you'd like to try your hand at showing and breeding your purebred dog. Conformation competition can be a very rewarding hobby for those who are enthusiastic about their favorite breed and dedicated to producing the finest-quality dogs. It only takes a few wins for some people to become hopelessly addicted to this pastime. For a dog lover, there is no thrill greater than seeing your pride-and-joy become a champion.

Keep in mind that dog showing and breeding can be expensive

Competing in conformation events can be fun and rewarding, but showing a dog is also time-consuming and expensive. To succeed, your Miniature Schnauzer may require professional grooming and extra training.

propositions. First, there is the often-substantial cost of a good-quality show dog. There are entry fees and travel expenses. You may also have to pay handler fees and training fees. Breeding expenses include stud fees, supplies, equipment, and veterinary expenses. Then, take all these expenses and multiply them, for it's a rare breed fancier who owns only one dog.

Before you become involved in showing, you should do plenty of research. Attend as many dog shows

FAST FACT

To become AKC champions, dogs acquire points each time they win at a dog show. The number of dogs entered in a show determines the point values awarded. A dog must earn a total of 15 points to become a champion, including at least two "major" wins that provided a minimum of 3 points each.

as possible so you can learn how they are run. Get expert advice on the purchase of a show dog. Talk to breeders, contact local breed clubs, and find a mentor who can instruct you in the specialized grooming required for show Miniature Schnauzers. Then enroll in some conformation training classes so both you and your dog can learn how to present yourselves as winners.

TRAVELING WITH YOUR MINIATURE SCHNAUZER

When you travel with your Miniature Schnauzer—whether by plane, train, or automobile—the safest way to transport your dog is in a crate. Airlines have varying rules for the size and type of pet crates they allow. Make sure to check before you buy your tickets.

Safety should always be of primary concern when you travel with your precious cargo. Make sure all vaccinations are up-to-date. As a precaution, bring along copies of vaccination records and your veterinarian's contact information in case your Miniature Schnauzer suffers an illness. Carry a current photo in case your dog gets lost. Most important, don't ever trust your dog off leash in a strange place, no matter how well trained he may be. Dogs can become frightened or confused in an unfamiliar environment, and they can easily forget their training.

If you plan to stay at a hotel or motel, always make lodging arrange-

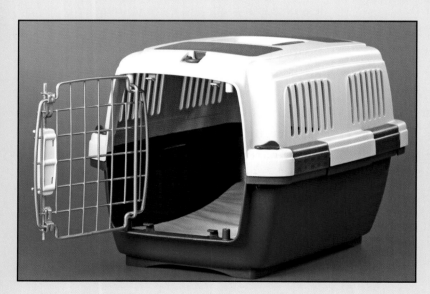 

Never allow your dog to ride in the car without some form of restraint. Ideally, the safest way to transport your pet is inside a hard or soft pet carrier.

ments ahead of time and ask whether the hotel is pet friendly. It won't be a very pleasant trip if you have to drive all over an unfamiliar place trying to find lodging that accepts dogs.

Finally, be sure to pack all your dog's necessary care items. You may not plan to groom your dog during your trip, but bring his brush anyway. You never know what kind of messy stuff your inquisitive Miniature Schnauzer might get into. Be sure to pack plenty of waste bags so you can clean up after your pet. And don't forget some toys to keep your furry pal busy. Traveling should be fun for him, too.

LEAVING YOUR MINIATURE SCHNAUZER AT HOME

When you have to travel without your best buddy, you'll need to arrange for his care. For short absences of a day or two, you might find a dog-loving neighbor, relative, or friend to look after your dog. For longer absences, however, you may want to hire a professional. Some professional pet sitters will come to your home several times a day to care for your dog. Others provide pet sitting services in their own homes. This may be more desirable if your dog requires the extra time and attention.

If your Miniature Schnauzer doesn't care for traveling in a pet carrier, a car harness provides a safe alternative. These harnesses typically work with your vehicle's seat belt to keep your pet in place during the trip.

Always evaluate a prospective pet sitter carefully. You will be entrusting him or her with something irreplaceable—your best friend. A professional pet sitter will set up an initial appointment with you to meet your Miniature Schnauzer and discuss the dog's needs. You'll know immediately if a pet sitter takes the "professional" part of the job title

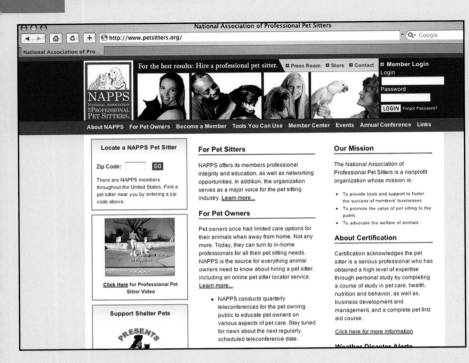

The Internet is a good place to find a pet sitter who is qualified to watch your Miniature Schnauzer while you are away. Sites like the National Association of Professional Pet Sitters, www.petsitters.org, can be searched using your zip code.

seriously. The sitter should have a contract outlining services offered, be insured and bonded, and be a member of a professional organization such as the National Association of Professional Pet Sitters (NAPPS) or Pet Sitters International (PSI).

Pay attention to how the sitter responds to your dog. Does the sitter seem knowledgeable about dogs and ask a lot of questions about your dog? Most important, do you feel comfortable with the sitter? If you have any doubts, look for another sitter.

Depending on your situation, a boarding kennel might be a better choice than a dog sitter. Today, the typical kennel is much more than a cold, hard doggy jail. Many kennels now offer soft bedding, toys, group playtime with other dogs, special feeding arrangements, and other amenities. Some boarding kennels house their charges in small, individual rooms instead of in kennel cages. They may offer a whole menu of optional services, including individual playtime with humans, group playtime with other dogs, canine massage, and even aromatherapy.

Depending on how much you're willing to pay, you can arrange for your dog to have his own luxury vacation. But regardless of how great they seem in their ads or over the phone, you should evaluate boarding facilities in person with the same scrutiny as you would a pet sitter. Are the facilities clean? Is soft bedding provided? Do the operators show an interest in your dog, or will your dog be treated like just another boarder?

CARING FOR YOUR SENIOR MINIATURE SCHNAUZER

Enjoying your Miniature Schnauzer doesn't have to stop when your dog starts coasting down the other side of the hill. Some Miniature Schnauzers retain their youthful energy and remain active in canine sports past the age of 10. Even if your dog shows signs of slowing down, there's much to enjoy in an older and wiser canine companion. Get the most out of this stage of your dog's life by providing the kind of care your senior dog deserves.

Your senior dog may be affected by a variety of age-related conditions. His digestive system may be more delicate; foods that he previously ate and loved may now cause stomach upset or diarrhea. His liver and kidneys may not function as well as they once did, and he may need to urinate more frequently.

The senses, too, tend to diminish with age. Your dog's vision may decline as the lenses of his eyes harden. His hearing may become notice-

A Miniature Schnauzer is generally considered "senior" once he reaches 9 or 10 years of age. With proper care, these dogs typically live 14 years or more.

ably impaired. His appetite and weight may decrease as his senses of smell and taste fade. Conversely, he may begin to gain weight due to a more sluggish metabolism and a decrease in activity.

You may notice that your aging Miniature Schnauzer experiences difficulty lying down or getting up, jumping onto the furniture, or climbing stairs. This is from the debilitating effects of arthritis.

Although senior dogs are not as active as they used to be, they still need plenty of exercise, proper food, and unconditional love from their owners.

Getting old is rarely easy, but that doesn't mean your dog's quality of life has to suffer. You can manage many age-related conditions with a few simple adjustments: talking to your dog louder so he can hear you, feeding him more frequently to avoid digestive upsets, or taking him out more frequently for potty breaks.

Other problems, such as kidney stones, diabetes, and heart disease, will require your veterinarian's help to manage.

Regular exercise is a great way to keep your older dog in good health. However, some precautions should be observed. Older dogs are not as tolerant of hot and cold temperatures, so you should limit outdoor excursions when the weather is uncomfortable. Older bones and joints are also more prone to injury, especially if your dog isn't as active as he used to be. Be very careful not to let your senior dog overdo it. Miniature Schnauzers are known for pushing themselves to the limit, especially when their prey drive has been excited. A daily walk is a great way to enjoy your venerable old friend and keep him fit at the same time.

SAYING GOOD-BYE

Sadly, there will probably come a time when you realize you can no longer maintain a good quality of life for your best friend. You'll know this is the case when your dog seems to get little enjoyment out of life, or when he is obviously suffering from pain or a chronic illness. Having to say good-bye is the highest price we pay for the love of a dog. But while it's hard to let go, it's also hard to see a precious loved one suffer.

Euthanasia offers the opportunity for our beloved pets to bypass the pain and suffering associated with a natural death. You, too, can avoid the heartache and trauma of watching your dog waste away or suffer pain when his life is drawing to an end. It may be the kindest thing you can do—both for your faithful companion and for yourself.

Euthanasia, a procedure performed by your veterinarian, consists of an intravenous injection of several drugs that erase pain and suppress vital organ function. Your dog will appear to go to sleep very quickly. His heart will slow, then stop. All this occurs in just a few short minutes. It is a peaceful process, and you'll know you've done the right thing for your old friend.

It's not easy to lose a cherished pet. The human-canine bond is perhaps the strongest of any interspecies relationship in the world. No matter how much you try to prepare for it emotionally, you may be surprised by the enormous sense of loss.

Grieving is a very personal process. The important thing is not to pay too much attention to what other people think. If preserving your pet's ashes in an urn makes you feel closer to your departed pet, do so. If you like the idea of planting a tree or making a garden stone so you can have a long-lasting memorial for your special friend, do so. If you want to donate to an animal shelter or veterinary university to honor your departed pet, do that.

Although it's great to review all the wonderful memories you and your Miniature Schnauzer have made together, it's not productive to dwell on your loss. So keep busy. Find projects to work on and make plans. When the pain slowly begins to subside, as it surely will, you'll realize how much your darling Miniature Schnauzer left with you that even death can't take away.

Organizations to Contact

American Animal Hospital Association
12575 West Bayaud Ave.
Lakewood, CO 80228
Phone: 303-986-2800
Fax: 800-252-2242
E-mail: info@aahanet.org
Web site: www.aahanet.org

American Canine Association, Inc.
P.O. Box 808
Phoenixville, PA 19460
Phone: 800-651-8332
Fax: 800-422-1864
E-mail: acacanines@aol.com
Web site: www.acainfo.com

American Dog Breeders Assn.
P.O. Box 1771
Salt Lake City, UT 84110
Phone: 801-936-7513
E-mail: bstofshw@adba.cc
Web site: www.adbadogs.com

American Humane Association
63 Inverness Dr. East
Englewood, CO 80112
Phone: 303-792-9900
Fax: 303-792-5333
Web site: www.americanhumane.org

American Kennel Club
8051 Arco Corporate Dr., Suite 100
Raleigh, NC 27617
Phone: 919-233-9767
E-mail: info@akc.org
Web site: www.akc.org

American Miniature Schnauzer Club (AMSC)
Mary Ann Shandor
2302 Cumberland Court, SW
Decatur, AL 35603-2617
E-mail: membership@amsc.us
Web site: www.amsc.us/index.php

American Working Terrier Association (AWTA)
Ann Wendland, Recording Secretary
15720 State Highway 16
Capay, CA 95607
E-mail: ratracejrt@gvni.com
Web site: www.dirt-dog.com

Association of Pet Dog Trainers
150 Executive Center Dr., Box 35
Greenville, SC 29615
Phone: 800-738-3647
Fax: 864-331-0767
E-mail: information@apdt.com
Web site: www.apdt.com

The Canadian Kennel Club
89 Skyway Avenue, Suite 100
Etobicoke, Ontario, M9W 6R4
Canada
Phone: 416-675-5511
Fax: 416-675-6506
E-mail: information@ckc.ca
Web site: www.ckc.ca/en

**Canine Eye Registration
Foundation**
1717 Philo Road
P.O. Box 3007
Urbana, IL 61803-3007
Phone: 217-693-4800
Fax: 217-693-4801
E-mail: cerf@vmdb.org
Web site: www.vmdb.org/cerf.html

**Canine Health
Foundation**
P.O. Box 37941
Raleigh, NC 27627-7941
Phone: 888-682-9696
Fax: 919-334-4011
E-mail: akcchf@akc.org
Web site: www.akcchf.org

Delta Society
875 124th Ave., NE
Suite 101
Bellevue, WA 98005
Phone: 425-226-7357
E-mail: info@deltasociety.org
Web site: www.deltasociety.org

**Humane Society
of the United States**
2100 L St., NW
Washington, DC 20037
Phone: 202-452-1100
Fax: 301-548-7701
Email: info@hsus.org
Web site: www.hsus.org

**The Kennel Club
of the United Kingdom**
1-5 Clarges St.
Picadilly
London W1J 8AB
United Kingdom
Phone: 0870 606 6750
Fax: 020 7518 1058
Web site: www.thekennelclub.org.uk

**National Association of Dog
Obedience Instructors**
PMB 369
729 Grapevine Hwy
Hurst, TX 76054-2085
E-mail: corrsec2@nadoi.org
Web site: www.nadoi.org

**National Association of
Professional Pet Sitters (NAPPS)**
17000 Commerce Parkway, Suite C
Mt. Laurel, NJ 08054
Phone: 856-439-0324
Fax: 856-439-0525
E-mail: napps@ahint.com
Web site: www.petsitters.org

National Dog Registry
P.O. Box 51105
Mesa, AZ 85208
Phone: 800-NDR-DOGS
Web site: www.nationaldogregistry.com

**North American Dog Agility
Council (NADAC)**
P.O. Box 1206
Colbert, OK 74733
E-mail: info@nadac.com
Web site: www.nadac.com

**North American Flyball
Association (NAFA)**
1400 West Devon Ave., #512
Chicago, IL 60660
Phone: 800-318-6312
Web site: www.flyball.org

**Orthopedic Foundation
for Animals (OFA)**
2300 East Nifong Boulevard
Columbia, MO 65201
Phone: 573-442-0418
Fax: 573-875-5073
Web site: www.offa.org

Pet Industry Joint Advisory Council
1220 19th Street, NW Suite 400
Washington, DC 20036
Phone: 202-452-1525
Fax: 202-293-4377
E-mail: info@pijac.org
Web site: www.pijac.org

Pet Loss Support Hotline
College of Veterinary Medicine
Cornell University
Ithaca, NY 14853-6401
Phone: 607-253-3932
Web site: www.vet.cornell.edu/
public/petloss

Pet Sitters International (PSI)
201 East King Street
King, NC 27021-9161
Phone: 336-983-9222
Fax: 336-983-9222
E-mail: info@petsit.com
Web site: www.petsit.com

Therapy Dogs International, Inc.
88 Bartley Road
Flanders, NJ 07836
Phone: 973-252-9800
Web site: www.tdi-dog.org

UK National Pet Register
74 North Albert Street, Dept 2
Fleetwood, Lancasterhire, FY7 6BJ
United Kingdom
Web site: www.nationalpetregister.org

**United States Dog Agility
Association, Inc. (USDAA)**
P.O. Box 850955
Richardson, TX 75085-0955
Phone: 972-487-2200
Fax: 972-272-4404
Web site: www.usdaa.com

Veterinary Medical Databases
1717 Philo Rd.
PO Box 3007
Urbana, IL 61803-3007
Phone: 217-693-4800
E-mail: cerf@vmdb.org
Web site: www.vmdb.org

World Canine Freestyle Organization (WCFO)
PO Box 350122
Brooklyn, NY 11235-2525
Phone: 718-332-8336
E-mail: wcfodogs@aol.com
Web site: www.worldcaninefreestyle.org

Further Reading

Degioia, Phyllis. *The Miniature Schnauzer*. Neptune City, N.J.: T.F.H. Publications, 2006.

Eldredge, Debra. *Dog Owner's Veterinary Handbook*. New York: Howell Book House, 2007.

Leach, Laurie. *The Beginner's Guide to Dog Agility*. Neptune City, N.J.: T.F.H. Publications, 2006.

Moustaki, Nikki. *Miniature Schnauzers*. Neptune City, N.J.: T.F.H. Publications, 2008.

Owens, Paul, and Norma Eckroate. *The Dog Whisperer: A Compassionate, Nonviolent Approach to Dog Training*, 2nd ed. Avon, Mass.: Adams Media, 2007.

Palika, Liz. *The Ultimate Pet Food Guide: Everything You Need to Know About Feeding Your Dog or Cat*. Cambridge, Mass.: Da Capo Press, 2008.

Internet Resources

http://amsc.us

The Web site of the American Miniature Schnauzer Club includes the breed standard, a list of reputable breeders, information about Miniature Schnauzer grooming and care, and links to local breed clubs.

http://www.aspca.org

The Web site of the American Society for the Prevention of Cruelty to Animals (ASPCA) provides valuable information for pet owners.

http://www.dogplay.com

This site has information on all kinds of games, sports, and other bond-building activities for you and your Miniature Schnauzer.

http://www.hsus.org

The official Web site of the Humane Society of the United States offers valuable information about pet adoption as well as general pet care tips.

http://www.petfinder.com

This Web site can help you find adoptable Miniature Schnauzers through shelters and rescue groups in your area.

http://www.uwsp.edu/psych/dog/dog.htm

Dr. P's Dog Training Web page provides links to dozens of training articles, many of which are written by experts in their field.

http://www.akc.org/breeds/miniature_schnauzer/

This page contains the American Kennel Club's description of the Miniature Schnauzer breed standard.

http://www.thekennelclub.org.uk/item/167

This page contains a description of the breed standard for Miniature Schnauzers as established by the Kennel Club of the United Kingdom.

http://www.westminsterkennelclub.org

This Web site includes breed information, showmanship videos, and details about the Westminster Dog Show.

Index

Numbers in **bold italics** refer to captions.

Contributors

JANICE BINIOK has written numerous articles and books on companion animals, including *The Poodle* and *The Yorkshire Terrier* for Eldorado Ink's OUR BEST FRIENDS series. As a former professional dog groomer, Janice has a particular fondness for the Miniature Schnauzer breed. She has an English degree from the University of Wisconsin-Milwaukee and is a member of the Dog Writers Association of America.

Senior Consulting Editor **GARY KORSGAARD, DVM,** has had a long and distinguished career in veterinary medicine. After graduating from The Ohio State University's College of Veterinary Medicine in 1963, he spent two years as a captain in the Veterinary Corps of the U.S. Army. During that time he attended the Walter Reed Army Institute of Research and became Chief of the Veterinary Division for the Sixth Army Medical Laboratory at the Presidio, San Francisco.

In 1968 Dr. Korsgaard founded the Monte Vista Veterinary Hospital in Concord, California, where he practiced for 32 years as a small animal veterinarian. He is a past president of the Contra Costa Veterinary Association, and was one of the founding members of the Contra Costa Veterinary Emergency Clinic, serving as president and board member of that hospital for nearly 30 years.

Dr. Korsgaard retired in 2000. He enjoys golf, hiking, international travel, and spending time with his wife Susan and their three children and four grandchildren.